The Travels of Herodotus

ABOUT THE BOOK

Two thousand, five hundred years ago, Herodotus singlehandedly created the concept of Western Civilization. Fortunately, because he found the world an inexhaustible source of fascination and delight, he is himself an inexhaustibly fascinating man. The father of history displayed all the modern techniques now associated with analytical journalism, television interviewing, film travelogues and historical research. Indeed, it is precisely his creation of these techniques which makes him our eternal contemporary.

The distinguishing qualities of Western civilized man—our constant wonder at the world, our insatiable thirst for understanding it, our passion for heritage and cultural origins and their preservation —all derive from Herodotus. We are direct heirs to his optimism and his fundamental belief that the marvellous multiplicity and diversity of all phenomena are subject to and worthy of human understanding.

Herodotus travelled throughout the known world and beyond in his unceasing quest for primary sources to substantiate his history of Western Civilization. Richard Lister has retraced Herodotus's footsteps through the ancient marvels of Persia and Babylon, Egypt and North Africa, Turkey, Russia, Greece and Italy, and at each halting place proves how amazingly accurate, thorough and professional were Herodotus's observations and research.

Wherever Herodotus travelled, he gathered information about local customs, religion, architecture, diet, medical practices, flora and fauna, politics. His observations were meticulous and his descriptions were made the more vivid by his friendly habit of interviewing everyone, from prostitutes and sailors, nomads and merchants, to scholars and priests, tyrants and princes. Richard Lister has written a fascinating biography which stands as an account of how our Western Civilization was formed by a single congenial genius.

ABOUT THE AUTHOR

R. P. Lister was born in 1914 and educated at Manchester University. He has written six novels (including *The Rhyme and the Reason, The Questing Beast,* and *One Short Summer*). His poetry has been published in *The New Yorker, Atlantic Monthly* and *Punch*. His travel and historical writings include *A Journey In Lapland, Turkey Observed, The Secret History of Genghis Khan*, and for Gordon & Cremonesi, *Marco Polo's Travels in Xanadu with Kublai Khan.*

BY THE SAME AUTHOR

NOVELS
The Way Backwards
The Oyster and the Torpedo
Rebecca Redfern
The Rhyme and the Reason
The Questing Beast
One Short Summer

TRAVEL
A Journey in Lapland
Turkey Observed

BIOGRAPHY
The Secret History of Genghis Khan
In Xanadu with Kubla Khan: Marco Polo's Travels

VERSE
The Idle Demon

HE TRAVELS OF HERODOTUS

R. P. Lister

With illustrations
by the author

GORDON & CREMONESI

Designed by Heather Gordon
Set in 12pt on 13pt Monotype Garamond and printed in Great Britain
at The Anchor Press Ltd and bound by Wm Brendon & Son Ltd
both of Tiptree, Essex

British Library Cataloguing in Publication Data

Lister, Richard Percival
    The Travels of Herodotus.
    1. Herodotus   2. Historians–Greece–1–Biography
    I. Title
    938'.007'2024   D56.52.H45   78–41259
LCCN: 78–041259
ISBN: 0–86033–081–8

Gordon & Cremonesi Publishers
London and New York
New River House
34 Seymour Road
London N8 0BE

CONTENTS

Maps

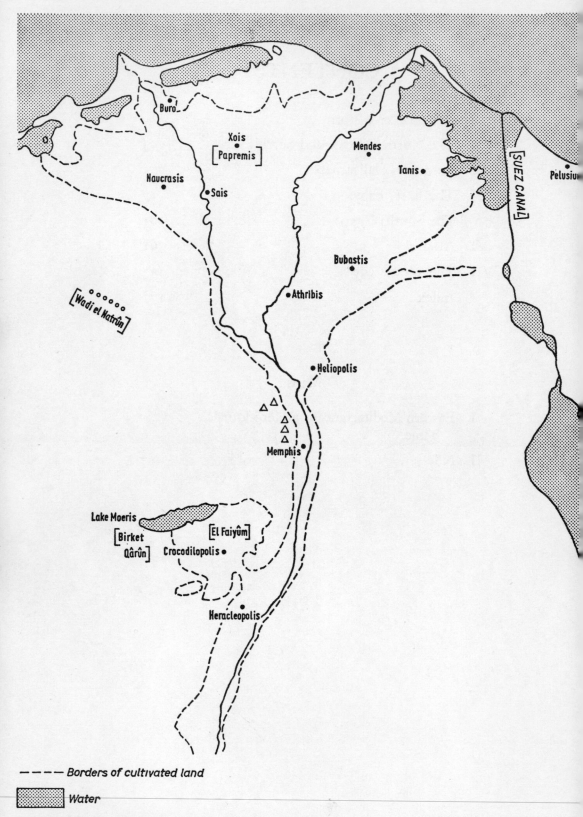

Buro

Xois
[Papremis]

Mendes

Naucrasis

Tanis •

Pelusiu

• Sais

[SUEZ CANAL]

Bubastis

• Athribis

[Wadi el Natrûn]

• Heliopolis

Memphis •

Lake Moeris

[Birket
Qârûn]   Crocodilopolis •

[El Faiyûm]

Heracleopolis •

– – – – Borders of cultivated land

Water

The courses of the Nile shown are the principal modern ones

A TRAVELLER IS BORN

I

The birthplace: Halicarnassus, a border area. How the Greeks came to Greece——emergence of classical Greece. Origins of the Persians——Cyrus the Persian conquers Croesus the Lydian——the Greek cities of Asia pay tribute to Persia——Cambyses invades Egypt——the throne usurped by Darius——Darius invades Greece——defeated at Marathon——death of Darius.

Herodotus born in Halicarnassus——Xerxes invades Greece——Artemisia the tyrant of Halicarnassus——crossing of the Hellespont——defeat at Salamis——Xerxes returns to Persia leaving Mardonius to carry on the war——Mardonius's army defeated at Plataea——Artemisia's grandson Lygdamis tyrant of Halicarnassus——liberation movement in Halicarnassus——Herodotus, implicated, flees to Samos.

HERODOTUS WAS BORN in 484 B.C. in Halicarnassus, a city on the west coast of Asia Minor. The town that now stands on the site of Halicarnassus is called Bodrum, a Turkish word meaning "cellar", and it is in Turkey. The region has been ruled by Turks for six or seven hundred years, and for some time now its population has been largely Turkish, though for a few centuries after the Turks began to rule the area it was recognizably Greek. Race in the biological sense has little significance in such matters, and in Asia Minor, as in Europe, descent is lost in confusion. The distinction between the Turks of Bodrum and the Greeks of Halicarnassus lies almost entirely in language and culture.

Herodotus was born at a time when Halicarnassus had been Greek for about the same length of time that Bodrum has now been Turkish. His ancestors who brought Greek language and culture to the city had done so by the same process by which the Turks brought their language and culture to Bodrum: by conquering their predecessors.

When Herodotus was born, Halicarnassus, though Greek by language and culture—at least as far as its ruling class was concerned; many of its inhabitants were Carians, Lydians and such—was, and had been for sixty years, under the rule of Persia.

This was in fact a border area. The Greeks had established a foothold there at a time when no group of people exerting wide-flung power had been in a position to resist or eject them. Even so, they had encountered resistance in pushing further inland, and it was for this reason that Greek settlements in Asia remained a mere fringe, clinging to the coast and hardly anywhere out of sight of the sea. Any major power springing up inland was likely to consider the Greek cities a desirable part of its empire, and take them over. The first power to do so had been the Lydians. The Persians, in conquering Lydia, took over the Greek cities at the same time.

The Greeks and the Persians were originally the same people: that is to say, the ancestors of the people who brought the Greek language and culture to Greece and those of the people who brought the Persian language and culture to Persia were, long ago, the same ancestors, speaking the same language and sharing the same culture.

The Greeks had been in Greece longer than the Persians had been in Persia. It was in about 2000 B.C.—fifteen hundred years before Herodotus was born—that the ancestors of the people who founded Greek civilization came to Greece from the north. They rode horses, drove horse-drawn chariots and had weapons of bronze. These advantages, together perhaps with some superiority of organization and a spirit of competitiveness or aggression, enabled them to establish their rule over the settled agrarian society which populated those countries already. Gradually they made their way southwards, down the Greek peninsula, across the isthmus to the Peloponnese, and across the sea to the islands.

After they had been there for five hundred years or so a brilliant Bronze Age civilization flourished on the Greek mainland. Its centres were a number of small towns containing, besides palaces, fortresses of great strength. One of these was at Mycenae in Argolis. It may have been the chief centre and has in any case given its name to the civilization and the period in which it flourished. The rulers spoke an early form of the Greek language; the people they ruled may have regarded them to a greater or a lesser extent as aliens. The Mycenaean culture was strongly influenced by that of Minoan Crete, which for a certain time had dominated the mainland. The origins of the Homeric legend date back to this period; the Trojan War took place some time before 1200 B.C., though in describing some of the incidents and characters of that war a few hundred years later Homer was probably about as accurate as Shakespeare was in dealing with the eleventh-century Scotland of Macbeth. Just as there was certainly a man called Macbeth who murdered a king called Duncan, there was certainly a city called Troy in Asia which was attacked by Greeks from Europe in the time of a king of Mycenae called Agamemnon; and the inaccuracy of both accounts in matters of detail may well be mitigated by the basic validity of the overall picture.

Some time after 1200 B.C. the Mycenaean civilization came to a fairly abrupt end. Many fortresses were destroyed and many settlements abandoned. The cause is obscure, but a revolt of the subject populations is a possibility.

A great deal happened in the four centuries following the fall of

Mycenae, but the exact sequence of events is unknown and is likely to remain so, though much may still be elucidated by archaeology. What is certain is that it was a time of confusion and movement of peoples. A fresh wave of invaders, the Dorians, entered Greece from the north. They were of the same stock as those who had preceded them and who had now been settled in the country for some centuries, but they were distant and unwelcome relations. The Dorians passed down the mainland of Greece to settle largely in the Peloponnese. Another wave of invaders, the Boeotians, settled north of Attica and the Gulf of Corinth.

Both before, during and after the Dorian and other invasions, large numbers of the previous settlers migrated across the Aegean to the west coast of Asia Minor, where they founded Greek cities. They found various peoples in possession and took over their lands by conquest. As is usual in such cases, it is difficult to tell exactly what happened, and to what extent the conquerors actually replaced the conquered. There was a degree of actual eviction, and a degree of actual enslavement; apart from these there were alliances, betrayals, marriages, concubinage, servitude, collaboration, slow processes of law and swift processes of force. Sometimes there are quite detailed accounts of who combined with whom to drive out whom, but even in these it is rarely easy to discern the numbers, nature and motivation of those involved.

In the eighth century B.C. the mists begin to clear. What emerges is recognizable as classical Greece. Somewhere along the way, in the preceding darkness, the use of iron has been discovered. The pantheon of Greek gods is in place. In the latter half of that century Homer, an Asiatic Greek like Herodotus, writes the *Iliad* and the *Odyssey*. The Greeks live not only in mainland Greece and the islands but in settlements around the shores of the Mediterranean and even the Black Sea. On the western coasts of Asia Minor, the people of the settlements are Aeolians in the north, Ionians in the centre, Dorians in the south; as if they had come straight across the sea from the nearest part of Greece, since this is roughly how they were situated on the mainland.

Herodotus, when he was born three hundred years later, knew himself to be a Greek, though this would not have been his word for it. There was no such thing as a nation-state; Greeks were Spartans, Athenians, Boeotians, Milesians. But the Halicarnassians had close ties with Greeks of the islands and of the European mainland, and they spoke the same language, or dialects of the same language. They shared a common way of life, worshipped the same gods, followed the same customs. Those who did not, who spoke a different language, they called barbarians: people who spoke as if they were stuttering, making noises like "bar-bar-bar".

The city was the independent unit of government. It ruled itself and the surrounding countryside, making alliances with or declaring war on other cities. Its citizens took an intimate and a vociferous part in the ruling of the city; though it must be remembered that the citizens formed only a small part of the population, being heavily outnumbered by women, children and slaves. Besides this, democracy was rare and short-lived, and freedom of speech was relative, as the fate of Socrates (a near-contemporary of Herodotus, being his junior by fifteen years) demonstrates.

Nevertheless, there was something distinctly and uniquely recognizable as the Greek spirit. It involved, among other things, an intellectual independence, a liveliness of mind, a curiosity about the world and how it worked. These may have arisen from a variety of causes, such as the way in which the landscape was chopped into small interesting fragments by the intermingling of land and sea; by the changeable but benignant nature of the climate; by the clarity of the air, the alternation of the land between harshness and fertility, or the constant moving and mingling of peoples during the period of migration. It may even be due in part to the institution of slavery, whereby members of the ruling class had a number of hands to aid them in the more mundane tasks needed for survival, without the massive availability of aid that might render them brutish or gross. It certainly benefited from an intrinsic self-confidence, a belief that Greeks were specially favoured by their relations, the gods.

However the Greek spirit arose, it was more effective than language in separating the Greek from his close cousin the Lydian, and even more so from his more distant relation the Persian. The spirit of intellectual inquiry is a fragile growth. Even in Greece at its apogee it infected only a minute proportion of the population. When Croesus, king of Lydia, invited all the wise men of Greece to his court at Sardis, he ran no risk of a sudden outbreak of scepticism and speculative daring among the Lydians, any more than Frederick the Great, when he invited Voltaire to visit him, risked an upsurge of Gallic acuity among the Prussians.

Medes and Persians were both Indo-European peoples, or Aryans, and they came into Persia from the north, just as their cousins came to Greece, but rather later. Reza Shah in the 1930s very properly ruled that Persia should be known by the name of "Iran", meaning "Aryan", since the Persians were only a part of the people, those living in the province of Fars, and the Iranians needed a more comprehensive name for the whole.

By 1500 B.C. Aryans were fairly widespread in the Near East, and because they had superior weapons and military talents they often formed a ruling class, dominating a subjected agricultural and pastoral society. On the whole, however, these forerunners tended to be absorbed into the indigenous population. It was not until about 1000 B.C. that the Aryan invaders came in such numbers as to impose their languages and customs on the people they conquered.

At this time the power of Assyria was growing. The kings of Assyria were harsh and cruel; fear and hatred are self-perpetuating, and the Assyrians ruled by terror. Subject populations were dealt with by mass deportation and mass murder. Ruthlessness is by no means admirable, but it can be effectual in the creation and maintenance of empires. Towards the end of the eighth century B.C.—about the time Homer was at work on the *Odyssey* in sunny Ionia—Sargon II ruled from his capital of Nineveh, no great distance from Mosul in modern Iraq, over Babylonia, Syria, Palestine and considerable areas of Iran. Under his successor Sanherib, Babylon revolted and was destroyed. Ionian mercenaries served in the armies that destroyed it. Under Asarhaddon, thirty years later, Egypt was conquered. In 645 B.C. Assurbanipal captured and destroyed Susa, the capital of the state of Elam, in the plains east of the Tigris, below the Zagros Mountains. Susa, rebuilt, later became the capital of Persia. Darius the Great built a palace there; now it is a village called Shush, notable for little but the nearby archaeological excavations.

Empires, fortunately for those members of humanity who are either rulers or subjects of them, do not last: the rulers become stupid with pride, the subjects from sheer desolation. The Assyrian Empire fell to its old enemies, the Babylonians, aided by some new ones, the Medes.

The Medes were a nation of Aryan invaders ruling over a non-Aryan population in western Iran. About 700 B.C., a confederation of Median princes was formed, and in 625 B.C. the Median chieftain Kashtaritu brought these into closer union to form the first Median state. The power of the Medes grew under his son Cyaxares, who succeeded him in 625 B.C. According to Herodotus, it was Cyaxares "who first organized the Asiatic armies by dividing them into separate units—spearmen, archers and cavalry. Previously the different arms had all been mixed up in a mob".

The Babylonians—now more commonly known as Chaldeans—rose up against the Assyrians, whose empire was beginning to be weakened by the familiar imperial complaints of dropsy, complacency and self-indulgence. The Medes joined with them to attack the Assyrians in 616 B.C. The Assyrians were aided by the Egyptians; nevertheless the Babylonians and Medes successfully invaded their territories, and in 612 B.C. the Assyrian capital, Nineveh, was destroyed after a siege.

The Babylonians went on to defeat the Egyptian army at Carchemish in 605 B.C. The Medes expanded their own territory in regions further north, advancing through eastern Anatolia until they came to the sphere of influence of the Lydians.

The Lydians were another Indo-European people ruling the whole of that western bulge of Asia Minor, with the trifling exception, at this time, of the Greek cities on the coast. They had not been powerful for any length of time, having taken over from the Phrygians (whose power had been destroyed by the Cimmerians) some fifty years or so earlier. The Lydians were a people noted for their commercial talents. They were widely credited with the invention of gold and silver coinage, and also of retail shops of the permanent kind, as opposed to markets. In this, as in other matters, the Lydians had a profound effect on the Ionian Greeks.

The Medes and the Lydians fought an inconclusive battle on the eastern frontiers of Lydia. The Medes called in the Babylonians as arbitrators, and a boundary between the two nations was fixed "for all time" on the river Halys, now known as the Kizil Irmak.

At this time Lydia was ruled by a king called Alyattes. He carried on frequent small wars against the Greek cities on his western coast. His success was limited, but the ultimate prospects were good. In 560 B.C., when Alyattes died and was succeeded by his son Croesus, the situation in the whole of the Near East seemed reasonably stable. In the south was the Babylonian Empire, stretching from the Gulf of Persia to the Mediterranean, and taking in Mesopotamia, Syria, Palestine and the Sinai peninsula. North of it the Median Empire stretched from the regions of eastern Iran south of the Caspian westwards to the river Halys. West of the river Halys was the kingdom of Lydia, and between it and the Median Empire the river formed an immutable boundary.

Immutable boundaries are notoriously short-lived, and the Halys was no exception. However, it was not only the boundary between the kingdom and the empire that lacked permanence. Within thirty-five years neither the kingdom of Lydia nor the empire of the Medes existed. With them had vanished the Babylonian Empire. All of these, and more, had been taken over by the Persians.

The Persians were another Indo-European people who had come to Iran at much the same time and from much the same area of central

Asia as the Medes, to whom they were closely akin in every respect. They had settled southwards of the Medes in Fars or Persis, the region lying north of the Persian Gulf. Under Astyages, the last ruler of the Median Empire, they formed a province of the empire. Herodotus says that Cyrus was the son of Astyages' daughter, whom Astyages had married to the Persian Cambyses. Cyrus may or may not have been Astyages' grandson; the truth of the story is disputed, and Herodotus says there were other stories, though he thought them less reliable. What is certain is that he was a prince of the Achaemenid line of Persian princes who revolted against Astyages and overthrew him, with the aid of the Medians themselves. Astyages, it seems, was unpopular with his subjects, possibly on account of his cruelty. However, overthrown princes tend to suffer from the posthumous propaganda of their successors.

During the Persian uprising against the Medes the king of Lydia, Croesus, took the opportunity to enlarge his own domains by the addition of some Median territory. He had already completed his father Alyattes' conquest of the Greek cities on the coast. Croesus, notorious then and ever since for his wealth, presided over a splendid and luxurious court, to which he once invited the leading sages of Greece, including Solon, the Athenian lawgiver. It seemed, to Croesus himself and to others, that he was destined to lead the Lydian people to ever-increasing power and glory.

Cyrus, having taken over the Median Empire and secured his own base, went to war against Lydia. He recovered the lost territories and besieged Croesus in his capital city, Sardis. The city fell; according to Herodotus, Cyrus began to burn Croesus alive, but when certain remarks of the victim concerning Solon aroused his curiosity he had the fire put out—not without difficulty, since it was well alight—and not only pardoned him but took him on as an adviser.

It was in 549 B.C. that Cyrus seized the throne from the Median Astyages. Two years later he conquered the kingdom of Lydia, and so, a little over sixty years before Herodotus was born, the Greek cities of Asia Minor, which had already been forced to pay tribute to the king of Lydia, began to pay it to Cyrus the Persian, who installed a satrap or governor in Sardis to rule this province of his empire.

After conquering Lydia, Cyrus turned against his recent allies the Babylonians, and conquered them. An unintended result of his victory was the freeing of the Jews from their Babylonian captivity. They returned home to Jerusalem and were later given permission (by Darius) to rebuild their temple, finishing it in 512 B.C.

Ten years after conquering Babylon, Cyrus was killed in battle against the Massagetae, the warlike nomads of central Asia, east of the Caspian, and he was succeeded by his son Cambyses. Plans had already been made for the invasion of Egypt, and Cambyses put them into effect. With him in Egypt, as a member of his bodyguard, was a certain Darius, son of the satrap of Fars. Cyrus had had his suspicions about Darius; it is said that he dreamed of the young Darius with wings on his shoulders that cast a shadow over both Asia and Europe.

Cambyses was a long time away in Egypt, and during his absence there was a struggle for power back in Persia. Exactly what happened in the summer and autumn of 522 B.C., eight years after Cambyses came to the throne, is not known. Cambyses certainly died; Darius, his successor, claimed that he died a natural death, and that a usurper claiming to be a son of Cyrus took over. Within a couple of months Darius was back in Persia and had had the usurper murdered and taken over the throne himself. Darius's account of the matter has some unsatisfactory features. He published it in the form of an inscription on a rock-face in Mesopotamia where it could (and can still) be seen by all, but it has never commanded universal belief.

Darius conceived of his empire as a multi-national community, rather than following the Assyrian model of a mass of subject peoples held down by brute force by a ruling race. Many of the satrapies were reserved for Persians, but some were held by non-Persians, and the higher administrative posts were by no means always held by Persians. In the same way, the army which at first had consisted mostly of Persians and Medes soon came to include men of various nations. The Persians ruled their empire but did not govern it in detail. The city-states of Ionia and Phoenicia, for instance, were almost independent, except that they had to pay taxes. They even issued their own coinage.

After putting down several internal revolts, Darius began to secure his empire. He visited Egypt, to deal with a dissident satrap there, and next mounted a punitive expedition against the Scythians east of the Caspian. He led an army eastwards and conquered as far as the valley of the Indus. During his reign a Greek admiral, Scylax, sailed down the Indus to the Indian Ocean whence he explored the sea-routes to Egypt.

Darius now turned his attention to the west. He crossed the Hellespont and subdued eastern Thrace; then, crossing the Danube, he marched up the west coast of the Black Sea against the Scythians. The Scythians, however, being a nomadic people, had little in the way of permanent settlements or non-portable possessions. They merely retreated before Darius into their illimitable hinterland, destroying everything they left behind. Darius, having followed them until his supplies were in danger of running out, had to turn back to the

Danube. However, although operations north of the Danube had shown little success, south of it Darius's satraps had extended Persian influence firmly over Thrace and Macedonia. The road to a conquest of Greece was secured.

The Greeks of Europe represented a permanent danger to the Persians, since they might bring aid and comfort to the Greeks living in Asia under Persian rule. Persian security therefore demanded the conquest of Greece. The danger was confirmed by a revolt in 499 B.C. of the Ionian cities. The Ionians received minimal support from Greece: Sparta refused any aid; Athens and the city of Eretria, in Euboea, sent a few ships and men. The revolt was successful for a few years, but the defeat of a Greek fleet off Miletus removed the possibility of further support from the Greek mainland. When the revolt was effectively crushed in 494 B.C. the Persians were able to begin subduing the rebellious cities one by one. In 492 B.C. a son-in-law of Darius, Mardonius, was made special commissioner in Ionia, with the aim of pacifying the inhabitants. He did much to reconcile the Ionian Greeks to their position as subjects of the Persian Empire by suppressing unpopular local tyrants and restoring some measure of democratic control of the cities to their citizens.

Darius now entrusted Mardonius with the command of an expedition against Athens and Eretria. Mardonius sailed with a sizable army, but the fleet ran into a major storm off the peninsula of Mount Athos and numerous ships were lost. Mardonius sailed home with the remnants.

Darius got together another fleet of six hundred ships and an army of three hundred thousand men and sent them off to Greece under the command of Datis, a Mede. Eretria was destroyed and its people taken into slavery, but on the way from there to Athens, in September 490 B.C., the army encountered eleven thousand Greeks at Marathon and was heavily defeated. The army had to retire into Asia.

Darius's preparations for another expedition, held up at first by an insurrection in Egypt, were halted by his own death. He was succeeded, in 486 B.C. by his son Xerxes, a rather impressionable man then in his thirty-sixth year.

Two years after the death of Darius, Herodotus the historian was born in Halicarnassus. Halicarnassus had originally been settled by Dorians from Troezen in the Peloponnese, but by the time Herodotus was born its speech and culture—that is, of the settler ruling class, as opposed to the local Carian population—was unmistakably Ionian. The city had a large sheltered harbour and a major command of the sea-routes south of Miletus, and became the capital of the small territory surrounding it. It was a part of the far-flung Persian Empire, coming under the governorship of the satrap whose seat was at Sardis, fifty miles or so inland from Smyrna, and once the capital of Croesus, king of Lydia.

For the first year or two of his reign Xerxes was busy in Egypt, quelling the rising that had broken out there in the last year of Darius's reign. His troops did great damage in the Delta. Next he had to put down another Babylonian revolt, during which he commanded the destruction of the statue of Marduk, the god of the city.

While Xerxes was taking these steps against his dissident subjects, preparations were being made for a massive expedition against Greece. Darius had recognized that the ultimate solution of the Greek problem, which was to take all Greeks into his empire, was not the minor operation it had seemed at first, but would need a major effort. Xerxes' enthusiasm for the project is thought to have been at first lukewarm, but his advisers insisted on its necessity, and Xerxes did not allow his early hesitations to diminish the scale of his preparations, which went on from the year 484 to 481 B.C.

The revolt in Ionia was by now a fading memory—it was thirteen years since its final suppression—and the steps taken by Mardonius had been so judicious and conciliatory that local representatives of the Persian government had no difficulty in recruiting large numbers of men of Greek stock for the expedition against their kinsmen in Europe. According to Herodotus, the contribution of Asiatic Greeks to the invasion forces was largely naval. Out of the 1207 triremes that made up the fleet, over three hundred were contributed and crewed by Dorians, Aeolians and Ionians from Asia and the adjacent islands under the rule of Persia. They carried Persians, Medes and Scythian mercenaries as marines.

Halicarnassus was at this time ruled by a hereditary tyrant who was, unusually, a woman. She was Artemisia, daughter of Lygdamis, a Halicarnassian, and a Cretan mother. She had married the tyrant of Halicarnassus, and on his death retained her authority as tyrant under the Persian satrap at Sardis.

Artemisia, loyal to her Persian masters, called for a major effort from the citizens of her despotate in support of the expedition against Greece. She raised five ships, with their crews, from Halicarnassus, Cos, Nisyra and Calydna.

The great army assembled by Xerxes set off from Sardis in 481, and at the same time the fleet that was to supply it from the sea on its over-land march set sail from the western coasts of Asia. Artemisia not only raised the five ships contributed by Halicarnassus, she now commanded them, as one of the few women naval captains known to history.

For the crossing of the Hellespont by Xerxes' immense army, two pontoon bridges were built. Both were destroyed by a storm. Xerxes, in his anger, commanded that the sea should be whipped. Pacified, perhaps, by this rebuke, the sea permitted the building of two more bridges and the crossing of the Straits. The army marched through Thrace and Macedonia, being met at suitable points by the fleet carrying supplies. A channel was dug through the isthmus at Acte so that the ships could cross into the Gulf of Singitikos without passing round the dangerous promontory of Mount Athos.

The progress of the army was ludicrously delayed by the intervention of a minute force of Spartans and Thespians at Thermopylae. These thousand men held up the entire Persian army for three days, in August 480. Having disposed of this irritant—the force was entirely wiped out but for one Spartan, who got back to Sparta, only to be met by reproaches because he had not died along with the rest—the Persians marched on, to occupy Boeotia and Attica and pillage Athens, whose inhabitants had removed themselves to the island of Salamis.

Xerxes now visited the fleet to consult its commanders about the advisability of attacking the Greek fleet which was sheltering in the narrow waters between Salamis and the mainland. With one exception all of them advised that the attack should be made. Artemisia, who had already achieved some reputation in the sea-battles off Euboea, advised the king to avoid naval action, since the Greeks were superior to the Persians in naval warfare, and instead to march with his army into the Peloponnese. The king, when Mardonius (reinstated to command this expedition) reported to him what Artemisia had said, appreciated the soundness of her advice, but decided to follow the majority opinion. His reason for doing so was that in the battles off Euboea—in which the Persians had suffered rather badly—his fleet had fought ineffectively because he was not present; now they knew he was watching the fight from the land they would certainly acquit themselves better.

The decision was a fatal one. The Greeks, by a cunning ruse of Themistocles, persuaded the Persian fleet to follow them into the narrow waters between Attica and Salamis. Here they were out-manoeuvred and heavily defeated. Artemisia distinguished herself in this battle, too, though principally by deceiving the Greeks into thinking the ship she commanded was a Greek one; this she did by turning and ramming one of her own ships, the one from Calydna, which fortunately for her sank with all hands so that nobody could accuse her of the crime. So, at least, Herodotus says: though his dislike of the pro-Persian dynasty that Artemisia represented may have prejudiced his account.

As a result of the defeat at Salamis the army was deprived of the naval support on which it had depended for its supplies. Mardonius advised the continuance of the struggle despite this, but Xerxes, having heard one piece of good advice from Artemisia already and failed to take it, asked her again what she thought. She suggested that he should go back to Asia himself, leaving Mardonius to carry on the war in Greece. Xerxes was delighted with this advice, since he wished for nothing more by now than to be safely back at home. He complimented Artemisia on her advice and commanded her to return to Asia, taking with her some of his bastard sons who were with him.

Xerxes marched back with all possible speed to Asia, reaching and crossing the Hellespont in forty-five days after parting from Mardonius in Thessaly. Mardonius, with the army the king had left him, resumed the proposed conquest of Greece. In the following year his army was defeated at Plataea, south of Thebes in Boeotia, and Mardonius was killed. On that same day the Persian fleet was defeated once again by a Greek fleet off Mycale in Ionia.

This was the end of Persian adventures in Greece: Xerxes devoted himself for the rest of his life largely to the building of Persepolis, the dynastic capital begun by his father Darius, and to the pleasures of palace life, until his assassination fourteen years later.

Artemisia, having left the bastard sons of Xerxes at Ephesus, returned to Halicarnassus, where Herodotus had by now reached the age of four.

Some time during the succeeding years she died and was succeeded by her son Pisindelis. He in turn was succeeded by his son Lygdamis, grandson of Artemisia and great-grandson of the first Lygdamis. During this time when Herodotus was growing up the political situation was much changed since the days of Xerxes' preparations for the great expedition against Greece. The European Greeks had followed up their naval successes against the Persians at Salamis and Mycale by an increasingly aggressive attitude. An Athenian fleet under Cimon carried out raids on the coast of Asia Minor, and the Greeks admitted the islands of the Aegean into their confederacy.

These circumstances provoked a new spirit of unrest in the Greek settlements of the coast. In the various cities conspirators met to discuss the possible overthrow of the pro-Persian tyrants ruling them and the setting up of truly independent city-states on the model of those of the Greek homeland and of their own original freedom,

with the support of forces from the mainland. Herodotus was aware
of these movements from his earliest days, and from his teens was
undoubtedly implicated in them. The movement appears to have
culminated in Halicarnassus in an uprising, or at least in what the
authorities considered to be the danger of an imminent uprising.
Herodotus was apparently involved in the plot and, at the age of
about twenty, had to flee for his life from his native city. A relative
of his, Panyasis the epic poet, was executed a few years later for his
part in political activities of the same kind.

Herodotus took refuge in the island of Samos, which was by then
free from Persian domination.

II

Greek ideas——the first Greek historians——Herodotus, his curiosity, impulsiveness and urge to travel——geographical work turned into history——sets off for the north ——the Hellespont——the Gallipoli peninsula, or Thracian Chersonese—— Cyzicus——Greek cities of the Propontis——Chalcedon——the foundation of Byzantium——the Thracian tribes——Greek and Thracian views on each other's customs——the Danube——the Bug and the Dnieper——the people of Scythia—— their origin and customs——the Agathyrsi——the Neuri——werewolves——the truth about the Scythians' neighbours now known——all were Scythians——the Alani——the Roxolani——Herodotus presumed to have visited Colchis—— Herodotus vindicated by modern excavations——Herodotus returns to Samos.

THE GREEKS ORIGINATED two revolutionary concepts that affected human history and have affected it ever since. One was political: the idea that men could organize the societies they lived in to permit a certain measure of individual freedom and open controversy, at least for some members of the society if not all of them. The other was the idea of philosophical and scientific enquiries made in a free spirit, with the sole desire to ascertain the truth.

Of these two, the political ideas first developed in mainland Greece, but the spirit of philosophical and scientific enquiry first grew and flourished most strongly in the Greek colonies in Asia. The effect of the new Ionia on Greece was immense and permanent. The impetus towards this kind of free speculation on the nature of the universe may have sprung in part from the stimulus of new lands and new climates acting on several generations of colonists: from the sense of adventure and discovery and freedom, the feeling that when an old country grew stale a new one could always be found. In part it may have come from liberation from dependence on the land, since leisure and liberty to think were conferred by the servitude of others.

It must be said however that very similar causes have not had the same effect on other colonists. On the contrary, colonial societies other than the Ionian have been mostly notorious for intellectual stagnation and a drabness of cultural life. West Indian planters had freedom, leisure, wealth and fresh prospects to gaze on, but to approach Jamaica hoping to find a mirror of Ionia would have been to invite disappointment.

The Ionian school of philosophers sprang up in Miletus, the south-ernmost city of the Ionian Confederacy, some forty miles north of Halicarnassus. Thales, one of the Seven Wise Men of Greece, was born there about 636 B.C. He was a philosopher and mathematician, and is reputed to have developed the art of mathematics so far as to have successfully predicted an eclipse of the sun which occurred in the reign of King Alyattes in Lydia.

The successor to Thales as leader of the Ionian school of philosophy was Anaximander, born in 610 B.C., an astronomer, mathematician and geographer. Following him came Anaximenes, who lived to a great age and was still alive when Herodotus was born, since he taught Anaxagoras in 480 B.C.: to such effect that Anaxagoras, who was then twenty—he was born in Clazomenae in 500 B.C.—went off to Athens, where he taught Euripides and Pericles, among others.

Besides being the birthplace of Greek philosophy, mathematics, astronomy and geography, the Ionian colonies were the home of the first Greek historians. One of the earliest was Cadmus, who lived about 540 B.C. in Miletus, at the time of its takeover by the Persians, and wrote a book on the early history of Ionia and the foundation of his own city. Another was Hecataeus, though he was primarily a geographer; one of his two known works was a description of Europe, Asia, Egypt and Libya, and he brought Anaximander's map of the world up to date. His other work was an account of the poetic fables and traditions of the Greeks. Hecataeus tried to dissuade the people of Miletus from rising against the Persians in 500 B.C., and when they insisted on doing so he gave them some advice on how to carry on the war. They ignored this advice also, and lost the war, although it is unlikely that they would have won it anyway.

As for Herodotus himself, many of the outstanding features of his character can be deduced from the circumstances of his early life, sparse though our knowledge of this is. It is clear from his book that he was intensely curious about everything, and that his curiosity extended beyond the facts themselves to the reasons underlying them. His premature revolutionary activities suggest that he was impulsive and a stranger to the spirit of caution. In his early years his major driving force was undoubtedly his desire to find out as much about the world as he could. He was widely read and highly educated, but the way in which he most enjoyed learning was not by reading but by travel, by making his own observations about the world and learning about its people, their characters and their histories, by meeting and talking with them.

One of the books that most impressed him as a student was the geographical work of Hecataeus, and that of Anaximander that preceded it. His own book purports to be a history, but it reveals his interest in geography by its numerous lengthy and detailed topographical descriptions. It seems fairly safe to assume that when he was living as a young man in Samos, looking for a way to make his mark in the world, his first resolve was to enlarge, correct and, if he could, outdo the work of Hecataeus by travelling as widely as possible and observing with his own eyes as many countries and peoples as he could.

At the same time, he was personally involved in the struggle against Persia to an extent that made it a major influence on his emotional and intellectual life. In the book he eventually wrote, geography and history are often seen struggling for supremacy. In the end history wins, but the sheer delight in place, in the physical shape and appearance of the world, is never absent for long from his work.

He travelled first to the north. This was in many ways the most mysterious of all the lands of which the eastern Mediterranean was the centre. Southwards lay Egypt, of which many Greek visitors had brought back reports; the connection between Egypt and Greece was long and ancient. All the countries to the east were now under the rule of Persia. Nearest were Caria and Lydia, familiar by hearsay if not by direct knowledge. Beyond them lay Phrygia, Cappadocia, Armenia, the kingdoms which had fought with varying fortunes against the Lydians and against the Medes and Persians. Westwards was Greece itself, and the Mediterranean, whose coastlands figured so largely in Greek legend, and where the Greeks had already by this time founded colonies as far to the west as Massilia, later known as Marseille.

To the north, on the contrary, was a land without history or geography, a wilderness with no cities, peopled, as far as was known, by savage nomadic tribes. There were scattered Greek settlements on the western and northern coasts of the Black Sea, but inland from these, and between them, lay the immense wastes of Thrace and Scythia, lands where there was no civilization of any kind, not even alien ones such as those of Persia or Egypt.

He sailed from Samos northwards, following the coast of Asia Minor, between Chios and the mainland and then past Lesbos, and entered the Hellespont. From the narrow entrance to the Straits you can see now, on the left hand, the Turkish memorial to the fallen at Gallipoli and, on the right, across the low plain, the small mound that was once Troy.

This was all territory newly liberated from the Persians. The first town they passed on the European side was Elaeus, at the extreme tip of the Gallipoli peninsula. The name of Gallipoli was unknown to Herodotus, who refers to the peninsula as the Chersonese, as was customary at the time among the Greeks; though formally it was known as the Thracian Chersonese, the Thracian peninsula, to distinguish it from the Crimea, which was called the Tauric or Scythian Chersonese.

About seventeen years earlier, in 481, Xerxes' fleet of triremes had lain at anchor off Elaeus to act as a base during the construction of the canal across the isthmus of Mount Athos. "From this base," as Herodotus says, "men of the various nations of which the army was composed were sent over in shifts to Athos, where they were put to the work of cutting [a] canal under the lash." He names the officers, two Persian noblemen, who were in charge of the operation. Natives of Athos were also pressed into service.

At Elaeus there was a temple to Protesilaus, a warrior of Thessaly who had been the first of the Greeks to be killed by the Trojans in the Trojan War. According to the *Iliad* he was the first of the Achaeans to leap ashore, but he fell to a Dardanian foe, leaving his wife in Phylace with lacerated cheeks and his house half-built. His wife was called Laodamia, and the couple were deeply attached to each other. When she received the news of his death Laodamia not only lacerated her cheeks, she also prayed to the gods to be allowed to speak to Protesilaus once again, if it was only for three hours. The request was granted, and Protesilaus was led back to the upper world by Hermes, the herald and messenger of the gods. He spoke to Laodamia, but when the three hours were up Hermes led him away again to the underworld, whereon Laodamia died. The house in Phylace, a little place in Thessaly, fifteen miles inland from the bay of Pagasaeus and lying north of Mount Othrys, remained unfinished, but at Elaeus, where Protesilaus was buried, a temple was built in his memory. It was what was known as a heroön, a temple dedicated to a hero, and was surrounded by elm-trees which, according to local belief, had been planted there by nymphs. It was said that as soon as they reached a height from which Troy could be seen, they died; fresh shoots then sprang up from their roots.

During the Persian occupation, as Herodotus recounts, the temple of Protesilaus had been subjected to exceptionally outrageous treatment by Artaÿctes, the Persian governor resident at Sestos, further up the Hellespont. Artaÿctes, on taking up his governorship, found that the temple at Elaeus contained many objects of immense value— gold and silver cups, bronze, rich garments and other things—that had been offered at the tomb by supplicants for the gods' favours or as thank-offerings to them. Artaÿctes, a man with an even greater love of wealth than most men, coveted these things, but he could not simply take them for himself, since if they were acquired as legitimate loot they would belong, like everything else, to Xerxes. So he wrote to Xerxes, saying: "Master, there is the house here of a Greek who made war on your country and met the death he deserved. Give me his house: it will be a lesson to men hereafter not to do as he did."

It is true that Protesilaus had invaded Asia, which the Persians now claimed as entirely their own by right, but he had done so in a remote age, several hundred years before the Persians had been so much as heard of, and his house, if he had one, was the one at Phylace that had been left unfinished long ago. This piece of acquisitive deception would have cost Artaÿctes his head if Xerxes had ever found out the truth about it, but as it turned out Artaÿctes did not survive long enough to confront his king.

Having received Xerxes' permission to take over the house of the Greek for himself, he cleared the temple of Protesilaus of all its valuable contents and had them taken to Sestos. He also ploughed up the sacred enclosure and planted crops there, and every time he visited Elaeus he kept his harem in the sanctuary.

Sailing up the straits from Elaeus, the next place Herodotus came to, on the opposite, Asian, shore, was the city of Dardanus. Long ago, in a very remote age, prior even to the building of Troy, a son of Zeus and Electra, Dardanus by name, had founded a city here which he called Dardania. From him were descended the Trojans, and among his descendants was Anchises, king of the city of Dardania. The goddess Aphrodite fell in love with Anchises because of his good looks, and by her he had a son, Aeneas.

According to the old traditions it was Aeneas who commanded the Dardanians in the Trojan forces led by Hector, son of Priam. And it was Aeneas, or one of the men he commanded, who slew the first of the Achaeans when they leaped ashore from their ships on their way to the war against Troy. The man he slew was Protesilaus, whose temple stood in the sacred enclosure at Elaeus. As for Aeneas, after the fall of Troy he fled to Italy, married the daughter of Latinus, king of the Aborigines, and founded the Latin race.

Centuries later, when in the time of the Greek migrations the Aeolian colonists landed here, they founded the city of Dardanus a little distance from the site of the ancient city of Dardania, now in ruins. In a later age still, the castles of the Dardanelles, built by the Turkish invader at this point where he crossed from Asia into Europe, gave their name to the straits; but to Herodotus this was the Hellespont, the sea of Helle, who fell into the sea hereabouts from the back of a golden ram and was drowned.

A little further up the straits they passed the city of Madytus, on the European shore, and beyond it, on the Asian shore, the city of Abydos. Abydos was founded by colonists from the Asian city of

Miletus. It was here that Xerxes commanded the building of a bridge across the straits for the crossing of his army. Two bridges carried on boats were built, crossing the Hellespont, here at its narrowest, from a point a little north of Abydos to a rocky headland opposite, between Madytus and Sestos. The width of the straits here was seven furlongs. One of the bridges was built by the Phoenicians, using flax cables, and the other by the Egyptians, using papyrus cables. When a violent storm sprang up and carried both bridges away, Xerxes, in his fury, commanded that the Hellespont should be punished by receiving three hundred lashes with whips, and besides this that the engineers who had carried out the work should have their heads cut off. Other engineers built two more bridges, using galleys and triremes lashed together and anchored by cables, 360 vessels being used for the bridge nearer the Black Sea and 314 for that nearer the Aegean. When the vessels were in position the cables holding them were hauled tight by wooden winches and across them from shore to shore was laid a bridge of planks covered with brushwood and, on top of that, trodden soil, with a paling along each side high enough to prevent mules and horses from seeing the water and taking fright at it.

When the bridge was finished, in the spring of 480 B.C., Xerxes came marching up from Sardis, visiting Troy on the way, and held a review of his army outside Abydos. He sat on a white marble throne on top of a hillock, looking across the shore to the Hellespont. The whole Hellespont, as Herodotus says, was hidden by ships, and all the beaches and plains of Abydos were filled with men. After watching a rowing match, which was won by the Phoenicians of Sidon, Xerxes suddenly burst into tears. When his uncle Artabanus asked him why, he replied that he was thinking how pitifully short was human life, since none of all these thousands of men would be alive in a hundred years' time.

On the day after the review Xerxes prayed that he might conquer Europe, poured wine into the Hellespont from a golden goblet, and flung the goblet into the Hellespont along with a golden bowl and a Persian short sword. The army then began to cross, the infantry and cavalry crossing by the upstream bridge and the pack-animals and servants by the downstream one. The Ten Thousand crossed first, the famous Immortals of the royal guard, all Persians and Medes, whose strength was kept up to its exact number by adding a new recruit every time a member died or was killed. The shafts of their spears were ornamented with golden pomegranates, and on this occasion they wore wreaths on their heads. They were followed by the troops of the numerous other nations that made up the bulk of the army, and after them came the horsemen, the sacred horses and

The great goddess Artemis, the multiple-breasted Diana of the Ephesians, was the omnipotent female deity of all Asia Minor and to whom Herodotus was particularly partial as he came from the Greek city at Bodrum, Halicarnassus, which was and is today adjacent to her main shrine at Ephesus. In Herodotus' time, Artemis was still the most powerful female goddess in the Greek pantheon even though she was not strictly of Greek origin and mainly of Greek adoption by colonial incorporation. She was goddess of fecundity, and of war; the latter attribute was gradually being taken over by her more domestic and chauvinistic mainland Greek counterpart, Athena, patroness of Athens. Artemis, as Herodotus was brought up to know her, was the same deity he found in Assyro-Babylonia under the names of Astarte, Ashtoreth, Ishtar, and in Egypt, as Isis, in North Africa as Neith, in Italy as Diana.

the sacred chariot. After these came Xerxes himself with his spearmen and his thousand horsemen. The crossing took altogether seven days and nights without a break.

A few months later the king was back again, after the defeat at Salamis on 20 October. His forty-five days of forced marches from Thessaly to the Hellespont had been made in bleak winter weather through a countryside denuded of supplies by the passage of his army in the spring. During the march the troops, as Herodotus says, "lived off the country as best they could, eating grass where they found no grain, and stripping the bark and leaves off trees of all sorts, cultivated or wild, to stay their hunger". Plague and dysentery attacked the army and many died, many more being left behind in Thessaly or Macedonia because they were too sick to march. When Xerxes and the remnants of his army reached the Hellespont they found that the two bridges had once again been shattered by storms, and crossed to Abydos by boat. In Abydos food was more plentiful, but this, instead of bringing relief to the army's long sufferings, brought yet more disaster, since many of the survivors died through the effects of over-eating on stomachs shrunken by starvation.

Further up the straits beyond Abydos, on the European shore, was Sestos, the seat of the Persian governor Artaÿctes who had desecrated the temple of Protesilaus. In legendary times there had been a priestess of Aphrodite in Sestos by the name of Hero. A youth of Abydos, Leander, was in love with her, and every night he swam the Hellespont to visit her, returning before daybreak. One stormy night he failed to make the crossing, being drowned on the way, and when, in the morning, his body was washed up on the coast near Sestos, Hero too threw herself into the waters.

Sestos was the strongest fortress in the region. Its inhabitants were principally Aeolian Greeks, but they had for long been under the rule of Persia and took part in its defence against the Greeks who came to attack the city.

After Salamis, the command of the Greek fleet was taken over from Themistocles by Xanthippus. He commanded the Athenians in 479 B.C. when they defeated the Persian fleet in the narrow straits between Samos and the Asian mainland, below the mountain and off the cape both called Mycale. He and his troops then began to clear the Persians out of their European conquests, and in the process they came to besiege Artaÿctes and his Persians, and his Greek subjects, in Sestos.

The siege was a prolonged one, and by the autumn even the besiegers were feeling the pinch to such an extent that they pressed their

B

officers to abandon the siege, but the request was refused and the siege continued. Inside the town the defenders were reduced to boiling and eating the leather straps of their beds. One night Artaÿctes and other Persians escaped by letting themselves down from the wall at the landward side of the town, where the enemy lines were weakest. Artaÿctes was pursued and captured not far from Aegospotami, further up the Hellespont. He offered his captors bribes, and promised to compensate the temple of Protesilaus, but Xanthippus and his men refused these offers. They took the Persian governor to a rocky headland which runs out into the Hellespont between Sestos and Madytus. Here they nailed him alive to a plank and hung him up on the headland, and stoned his son to death before his eyes. They then set sail for Athens, taking with them the cables of Xerxes' bridges to dedicate as an offering in their temples.

Xanthippus, incidentally, was married to a woman called Afarista, who dreamed during her pregnancy that she gave birth to a lion. A few days later she became the mother of Pericles; this was about 490 B.C.

Leaving Sestos and sailing northwards up the Hellespont, on the left was the mouth of the Aegospotami, or Goat-river, where Artaÿctes the Persian was captured, and on the right the town of Lampsacus. This town, on the Asian shore, was a Phocaean colony and the chief seat of the worship of Priapus. It was also the source of supply of the wine provided by the Persian king Artaxerxes for Themistocles when he fled to Persia in his old age. It is now called Lapseki, and almost opposite it is the town of Gelibolu, or Gallipoli.

After Lampsacus the Hellespont begins to broaden out into the waters of the Sea of Marmara, then called the Propontis. On their right, as they crossed the broadening sea, was the island of Proconnesus, the Fawn-island, so called because deer used to swim out there from the mainland to deliver their young in the fawning season. It was also famous for its marble quarries, from which it was given the name Marmara, from the Greek *marmaros*, a sparkling rock, which in turn comes from the verb *marmairein*, to sparkle. Beyond it they could see Cyzicus, which was then an island. It was connected by bridges across a narrow strait to the mainland of Asia Minor, at that time the Persian province of Mysia. In the following century, in the time of Alexander the Great, a mole was built to replace the bridges, and the resultant silting led to the formation of the present isthmus. There was a great and ancient city on Cyzicus, bearing the same name, founded by Pelasgians from Thessaly and later colonized by the Milesians; it flourished for more than a thousand years after Herodotus's time, until it was devastated by the Arabs in the seventh century A.D.

Further along the Propontis, on the Thracian shore, they passed the cities of Perinthus, founded by the Samians about a hundred years earlier, and Selymbria, founded, like Byzantium, by the Megarians, but before their foundation of that city. As elsewhere along these coasts, the cities were Greek, but the vast hinterland was still occupied by the wild Thracian tribes.

Standing out to sea to round the point where Yeşilköy and the airport of modern Istanbul now stand, they could see, twelve miles ahead, the opening of the Bosphorus. From here the modern traveller, sailing across the Marmara from the Hellespont, sees the minarets and domes of Istanbul riding up the ridge from Topkapi, the Old Seraglio; but when Herodotus and his fellow-travellers came this way all this was in the remote future. Even the other landmark for sailors, the statue of Zeus Ourios by Philo, that stood on the shores of the Propontis near Chalcedon, was not put up there until a hundred and thirty years later, in the time of Alexander the Great. Byzantium was little more than a hundred years old, and beyond it, across the mouth of the Bosphorus on the Asian shore, was the city of Chalcedon.

Chalcedon was founded by a colony from Megara in 685 B.C. on the site of an old Phoenician trading station that had existed there for the preceding three hundred years. It is known now as Kadiköy, one of the Asian suburbs of Istanbul, just south of Haydarpaşa. More than twenty years after the Megarians had founded their colony at Chalcedon, the famous navigator Byzas, reputed to be a son of Poseidon, set out from Megara, like the men of the previous generation, to found a city for himself. Before doing so he went to ask the oracle at Delphi where he should found it. She replied, "Opposite the blind." Failing to understand this reply, Byzas set out as the others had done, round Sounion, across the Aegean and through the Hellespont; and on the opposite side of the Propontis, not far from his cousins in Chalcedon, he found this miraculous site, provided by nature with a perfect sheltered harbour—the Golden Horn—and easily defensible from the landward side. The Chalcedonians, accused of being the blind referred to by the oracle for choosing to build their city where they did when a much better site was visible just across the water, could adduce various advantages of wood, water and pasture, but succeeding generations have considered that Byzas had the stronger case. The origin of this legend is, incidentally, dubious. According to Herodotus himself, it was Megabazus, a Persian, who said the men of Chalcedon must have been blind to found their city where they did.

At this time Byzantium, the Megaran colony on its splendidly situated and easily defensible spit of land between the Golden Horn and the Marmara, was eight miles in circumference. It had been liberated from the Persians a mere thirteen years before Herodotus's arrival, by Pausanias the Spartan, in 477 B.C. During the Persian invasion the other Greek cities had given Athens little support, but after Salamis, when the tide of war had turned, they sent contingents to aid in the struggle. The citizens of Sparta sent Pausanias with an army of five thousand fighting men, each one attended by seven helots. He commanded the army that defeated Mardonius at Plataea, and, after commanding the fleet that drove the Persians out of Cyprus, took his army to the liberation of Byzantium. His success in these activities led, as is not uncommon, to the inflation of his self-esteem beyond reasonable limits, and he decided to aim at ruling the whole of Greece. He wrote to Xerxes offering to marry his daughter and, with the aid of Persian troops and money, to bring Greece under his power and rule it as tyrant under the Persian king.

Xerxes agreed, but the correspondence between them was at length intercepted and Pausanias, hearing that he was about to be arrested by the ephors, the Spartan magistrates, took refuge in the temple of Athena Chalcioecus. The ephors promptly tore down bits of the temple and walled him up in it, with the assistance, so it is said, of Pausanias's aged and infuriated mother. He was taken out just before he died, in order not to pollute the sanctuary.

It was the arrogance of Pausanias at Byzantium, as much as his treachery, that led many Greek states outside the Peloponnese to favour the predominance of Athens over that of Sparta, with the consequent rise to power of the Athenian confederacy that was the first stage in the development of the Athenian empire.

The name Bosphorus means "Oxford", from the Greek *bos*, an ox, and *poros*, a passage, and the name was used for various straits; though this particular one was too wide to be forded by an ox at any point. Darius crossed the Bosphorus by a bridge, on his invasion of Europe that led to his defeat at Marathon. Herodotus says he did not know where the bridge was, and speculates that it may have been half-way up the straits. It seems probable that it was somewhere around Bebek, where the castles of Europe and Asia, Rumeli Hisar and Anadolu Hisar, face each other across the straits. The bridge had been destroyed long before Herodotus got there, and he gives no information about it except that it was designed by a Samian called Mandrocles and that Darius was delighted with it. It was presumably a bridge of boats like those erected across the Hellespont by the command of Xerxes. Darius had two marble columns erected nearby to commemorate his crossing, bearing inscriptions detailing the various nations over which he had dominion and which contributed levies to his army. This numbered 700,000 men, according to Herodotus, with 600 ships. The two marble columns, one inscribed in Assyrian and the other in Greek, were later removed by the people of Byzantium to be used in that city to build the altar of Artemis the Protectress, but the plinth, so Herodotus says, was left lying near the temple of Dionysus.

At the top end of the Bosphorus it opens out into the Black Sea. Here there were two rocky islands, the Cyanean Islands or Cyanean rocks. According to Greek mythology these were once movable, so that they rushed together and destroyed any ship that tried to pass between them; but after the *Argo* successfully passed through, under the captaincy of Jason, "the rocks were now rooted for ever in one spot", as Apollonius says in the *Argonautica*.

Here Darius, on his way to invade Scythia about 508 B.C., seated himself by the temple that stood by the straits at their northern end, in order to look over the Black Sea. It was a sight worth seeing, as Herodotus, who viewed it from the same spot forty-four years later, rightly says. Pausanias, liberator and later oppressor of Byzantium, also went to look at the view there, and set up a brazen bowl to commemorate the occasion.

Herodotus goes somewhat astray in his estimates of the size of the Black Sea, which he believed to be larger than the Mediterranean. He estimates its length as 1400 miles, basing this on the fact that it would take nine days and eight nights to sail from the Bosphorus to Phasis, the town at the mouth of the river that runs through Colchis at the extreme eastern end of the Black Sea. In fact it is about 910 miles at its longest, from the Gulf of Burgas to the mouth of that river. His estimate of its width, 405 miles at its widest point, is nearer the mark, but even more strangely he assumes the Sea of Azov to be not much smaller than the Black Sea proper: "the Black Sea is connected with a lake nearly as big as itself, called Maeotis, or Mother of the Pontus". He reckoned that the Black Sea was at its broadest, from north to south, between Sindica and Themiscyra: Sindica being somewhere near Taman at the entrance to the Sea of Azov, and Themiscyra a city at the mouth of the river Thermidon in the country of the Amazons, in Pontus, east of Amisus (now Samsun) and certainly near if not precisely coinciding with the modern Terme, east of Çarşamba. In locating the greatest width of the Black Sea at this point Herodotus is not so far out, though in fact it is a trifle broader further west, between Odessa and Akçakoca, west of Zonguldak.

As Herodotus journeyed northwards up the Black Sea, Thrace lay on his left. There were a few Greek settlements along its coast—Salmydessus, Apollonia and Mesembria south of Mount Haemus, the Balkan Mountains, in what is now Bulgaria; Odessus, the modern

Varna, north of the Balkan Mountains; and Istria, in what is now
Romania—but inland it was a wild country populated by wild tribes.
The Persians had subdued it, but only in the sense that they ruled the
coastal cities, and were able to march through the interior with large
armies. It was not a country through which a single unescorted
stranger could travel, and it speaks much for Herodotus's persistence
that on one or two occasions he penetrated it. For the most part it is
safe to assume that he travelled up its coast, by sea, staying at the
coastal cities, enquiring about the conditions inland and the tribes
that lived there, and travelling inland to visit those tribes himself
when he was assured that for the time being at least they were peace-
ably inclined, and with a suitable escort of experienced travellers and
interpreters, if not of armed guards.

He describes how Darius, having sailed up to the top end of the
Bosphorus and viewed the Black Sea, then returned to cross the
Bosphorus with his army and to march overland through Thrace to
the sources of the Tearus, which is two days' journey both from
Perinthus on the Marmara and from Apollonia on the Black Sea. It
seems reasonably certain that the sources of the Tearus were one of
the regions of inland Thrace that Herodotus visited in person, since
his description has an immediacy which could hardly have been
acquired by hearsay.

The Tearus was a tributary of the Hebrus, the principal river of
this part of southern Thrace, which flows into the Aegean not far
from Cape Sarpedon, where the great fleet of Xerxes anchored to
wait for his army. The Hebrus was noted in Greek legend; it was on
its banks that Orpheus was torn to pieces by the Thracian women,
maddened by Bacchanalian orgies. His head was carried down by the
river to the sea, to be buried later in Lesbos. The river was much
associated with the worship of Dionysus, in whom Herodotus took
a lifelong and somewhat nervous interest. Dionysus was a local god,
having been brought up by the nymphs of Mount Nysa; his worship,
which was accompanied by orgiastic rites, was first established in
Thrace.

The Tearus rose in what are now called the Stranca Mountains,
running roughly parallel with this south-western corner of the Black
Sea coast. Thirty-eight springs issuing from the same rock, some of
them hot and others cold, united to form the infant river. Its waters
were regarded locally as the best in the world for curative properties,
being especially effective for the treatment of scab in both men and
horses. Darius stayed here for three days, and was so charmed with
the place that he had a pillar erected there, inscribed with a typically
pompous message: "The springs of the Tearus, finest in action and

noblest in appearance of all rivers, were visited in the course of his march against Scythia by Darius, king of Persia and of the whole continent, finest in action and noblest in appearance of all men."

If Herodotus visited this place, as seems likely, he may have done so by travelling inland to it from Salmydessus, the nearest Greek city on the Black Sea coast, or from Apollonia, though, as he says, this is two days' journey away; or he may have visited it on a later journey, travelling up the two days' journey from Heraeum, near Perinthus on the Propontis. It is possible, though, that he followed the same route as Darius in this part of his journey, returning down the Bosphorus to travel overland to the sources of the Tearus. From here Darius and his army marched on to the north-west until they came to the river Artiscus, where he commanded all his men to deposit a stone in certain spots as they passed by, so that in this region great hills of stone were left behind along the way his army had passed.

Herodotus, however he reached the place, descended the north-eastern slopes, possibly to Apollonia. In this way he would avoid sailing along this stretch of the Black Sea coast, which from the mouth of the Bosphorus as far as Apollonia and Mesembria was dangerous because of shallows and marshes, so that the inhabitants found wrecking a profitable way of life.

Apollonia was in fact the first city of any importance. It was a Milesian colony, noted for a celebrated temple of Apollo. Mesembria, further up the coast, beyond the Gulf of Burgas near Thynia, was a colony founded by the inhabitants of Chalcedon and Byzantium —themselves originating from Megara—in the time of Darius, and hence at the time of Herodotus's visit it was barely a quarter of a century old.

Herodotus had a poor opinion of the Thracian tribes in the neighbourhood of Salmydessus and of Apollonia and Mesembria, who were called the Scyrmidae and the Nipsaeans. Apart from their wrecking tendencies, they had surrendered without a fight to Darius on his march north. The Getae, who lived further north, between the Haemus Mountains and the Danube, were a different matter. They were, he said, the most manly and law-abiding of the Thracian tribes, and, having fought fiercely against the Persian king, were defeated by him and taken into slavery. Many, however, must have escaped this fate by simply disappearing into the trackless hinterland, the privilege of nomadic people when defeated in battle.

The Getae worshipped a god that some of them called Salmoxis, though others knew him as Gebeleizis. They believed that they never really died, but went to join this god. Every five years they would choose one of their number by lot and send him to Salmoxis with a

list of their requirements. The man chosen was tossed up into the air
in such a manner that he fell on to the points of javelins held upright
by other members of the tribe. If he was killed this was a sign that
Salmoxis was in a good mood. If he survived this showed that he was
a bad character, and the god did not want him. The Getae would up-
braid him for his poor moral qualities and send another tribesman to
Salmoxis.

The Getae acknowledged no other god but Salmoxis, and during
thunderstorms they used to shoot arrows at the sky as a threat to the
god of thunder and lightning, who was usurping privileges that
properly belonged to Salmoxis alone. There were other gods in
Thrace, however, and Herodotus mentions those of war, of wine and
of hunting, equivalent to the Greek Ares, Dionysus and Artemis.
The tribal kings worshipped Hermes, the messenger and inventor of
the lyre, god of the road and all travellers, and giver of wealth and
good luck. The correspondence between local Thracian gods and
those of the Greeks may not have been as close as Herodotus imagines;
he tends here, as in other parts of the world, to give the names of
Greek gods to local gods possessing more or less the same attributes.
It is a similar process to that by which in a later age the attributes of
the Greek Artemis were transferred to the Roman Diana, and even
to the many-breasted fertility goddess of Asia Minor, who lived on in
disguise as Diana of the Ephesians.

From the coastal regions where the Getae, the Scyrmidae and the
Nipsaeans lived, Thrace extended westwards for something in the
order of 250 miles to the borders of Macedonia. From south to north
—from the Aegean to the Danube—it was little more than 185 miles
in width. It was not in fact an immense tract of land, but it contained
a large number of different tribes, and Herodotus goes so far as to
describe it as the most populous country in the world with the exception of India. He thought that if the Thracians could combine under
one ruler they would be the most powerful nation on earth.

They were a warlike people, to such an extent that the plunder
obtained in war was regarded as the only respectable source of income. Work was despised among them; the idle man was looked on as
the highest type of man, and the agricultural labourer as the lowest.
Another mark of distinction was tattooing, which showed a man
to be of high birth, lack of tattooing being the sign of the ill-
born.

It was the custom among them for a man to have many wives.
When a man died, his wives disputed among themselves to decide
which of them had been the most loved by the husband, the verdict
being given, after hearing all the evidence, by the late husband's

friends. The winner, after having been praised by all, was ceremonially slaughtered by her next of kin and buried by the husband's side. The losing wives, who were not granted the privilege of being killed, mourned their disgrace.

When a rich man died, his body was laid out for three days prior to burial. There was a preliminary period of mourning, followed by a feast. The body was then buried, either with or without cremation; a mound was raised over it and organized games were held, the most valuable prizes being given to the winners of single combat.

The Thracians customarily sold their own children to foreign merchants for export. No control was exercised over young girls, who were allowed to do whatever they pleased, sleeping with any man if they were inclined to, but once a man obtained one of them as a wife—which he did by purchase from her parents—he kept the strictest watch over her. According to Horace, the Thracians of his day were great drinkers, much given to violent quarrels in their cups. The Trausi, a tribe flourishing inland from the Scyrmidae, in the region where Adrianople later stood, had a custom which Herodotus describes as special to themselves but which seems to sum up much of the general Thracian outlook on life. When a baby was born, the family sat round and mourned, contemplating all the suffering that it would have to endure in this world; but when someone died they buried him with rejoicing, telling each other how happy he was now and how many more miseries he might have suffered if he had not escaped.

It is clear that the view taken by Herodotus of Thracians and Thracian customs was not entirely free from a tinge of what would now be called colonialism. Penetrating into the dark sub-continent of Thrace in the fifth-century-B.C. equivalent of a pith helmet, he saw the peculiarly un-Greek surface manifestations of Thracian life, and failed to observe the complexities of the culture that gave rise to them. This is far from unusual, but it is slightly surprising in view of the close relations in many respects between Thracian and Greek culture. The connections between Thracians and Greeks were long and intimate, as is instanced by the Thracian origin of the cult of Dionysus, who had an oracle high up in Mount Rhodope, and by the Thracian origin of such eminent Greek heroes as Orpheus and several other early poets, and Eumolpus, founder of the Eleusinian mysteries. Some Greek customs must have looked as comical or repulsive to Thracian eyes as Thracian customs did to the Greeks, and they had some justification for regarding themselves as in no way inferior. However, it is generally true of human beings that those who are most perceptive of the defects of other societies or social groupings tend to excuse or overlook the defects of their own. The Greeks were undoubtedly more knowledgeable in some ways than the Thracians, and in some ways more agreeable, and had more influence in moulding the modern world, which is no undiluted recommendation. On the other hand, though the Thracians sold their children, it was the Greeks who bought them.

In Sparta, the ephors selected young men to go around the country-side secretly at night, killing helots. In Athens, the breeding of slaves was discouraged, since it was cheaper to buy slaves than to rear them. A slave giving evidence in a court of law was required by law to be tortured, since his evidence given solely on oath could not be believed. Aristotle held that slavery was justified because some races were free and others slaves by nature. The latter category included all barbarians, that is to say, all who were not Greeks. Plato held that no Greeks should be enslaved by Greeks, but otherwise voiced no objection to the institution of slavery. All of which prompts the reflection that the Greeks, with all their admirable qualities, were no more qualified than any other men, ancient or modern, to accuse another nation of barbarism.

Herodotus gained other information on this visit about the Thracians in general and about individual tribes, some of which was confirmed by later visits to the Aegean regions of Thrace. He gives few details of Thracian domestic life or economy, beyond mentioning that they made clothes of Scythian hemp, which so closely resembled linen that people who had never seen that kind of hemp would think they were made from flax.

Beyond the Trausi there was a tribe called the Satrae that in Herodotus's time had never been reduced to subjection owing to the difficulty of the terrain in which they lived, the high mountain country in the western part of the Rhodope range, the Pirin and Rila mountains, densely wooded and often covered with snow. In these mountains, called in those days Pangaeum, there were gold and silver mines, some of them worked by other tribes but mostly by the Satrae.

It was in the territory of the Satrae that the oracle of Dionysus was to be found, on the highest mountain range. The Greek gods did not communicate directly with man by the time of Herodotus; their intentions or prognostications were communicated in more or less cryptic language to a medium for transmission to the supplicant. At Delphi they were uttered aloud by the Pythoness on her tripod, when she received them from the god in a trance, and were taken down in writing by the priestess. The procedure differed somewhat at different shrines, and all that Herodotus says of this one is that there was a priestess, as at Delphi, to deliver the oracles. He remarks that these were not more involved than the Delphic oracles; possibly a slightly caustic aside, since by his day the utterances of the Delphic oracle, which had always been somewhat slanted in favour of the Doric people, became so manifestly pro-Spartan that those, like Herodotus, whose sympathies lay rather with the Athenians began to lose all respect for it.

Westwards again from these mountains, the river Strymon—still called Struma—flows down from its source near Dimitrovo in Bulgaria, a dozen miles or so south-west of Sofia, to the sea in the Gulf of Strimon just east of the Mount Athos peninsula. On its way down to the sea it broadens out, just south of the frontier, to form a lake, known in Herodotus's time as Lake Prasias. Here there was a tribe of lake-dwellers who built their houses on the lake itself, driving piles into the lake bottom and erecting on top large platforms on which several huts were built. The platforms were reached from the shore by narrow plank bridges. Each man had his own hut for himself and his family, with a trap-door opening on to the water beneath. Fish were so abundant in the lake that all that was necessary to catch them was to let down an empty basket on a rope through the trap-door. When it was pulled up again a minute later it would be full of fish. Even horses and other pack-animals were fed on them. Children were prevented from falling into the lake by a cord tied round the leg. The men of this tribe married several wives each, and the custom was that a man should drive in three fresh piles for every wife he married, so that an ample supply of new building-space was always assured.

There were silver-mines in the neighbourhood that, according to Herodotus, later produced a talent of silver a day for the treasury of Alexander I of Macedon. Other ancient writers mention the large numbers of cranes to be seen on the banks of the Strymon, but Herodotus ignores these.

Further down towards the coast, the numerous Thracian tribes living between Mount Athos and the Chersonese were regarded as being appreciably more civilized than those of the interior, their manners having been softened by long contact with Greek colonists. They had been in contact in recent years with an even wider world, when the Great King, Xerxes, came marching along this coast with his immense army, bound for the invasion of Greece. When it came to crossing the Strymon, the Magi who accompanied the army tried to propitiate the river by a sacrifice of white horses and other magical tricks, as Herodotus calls them. When these had all failed they discovered that there were bridges further upstream at a place called Nine Ways, and the army crossed by these. Nevertheless, on hearing the name of the place, the Magi buried alive there nine Thracian boys and nine girls; burying people alive being, as Herodotus remarks, a Persian custom.

The route by which the Great King travelled was, when Herodotus visited that district, regarded with reverence by the local Thracians, who never ploughed it up or sowed crops where he had passed.

The northern boundary of Thrace was the Danube, which Herodotus describes as the mightiest river in the world. It rises, he says, among the Celts, who are a people living beyond the Pillars of Hercules and the most westerly of all European nations after the Cynetes, an unidentified people perhaps living in Spain. Having traversed the whole continent, it divides into five major channels and flows into the Black Sea near the Milesian colony of Istria.

One striking feature Herodotus noted of the Danube was that the volume of its waters never varied, summer or winter. He believed that the reason for this constancy of flow was that the increased rate of evaporation of its waters in the summer was balanced by the increased flow from the tributaries resulting from the melting of the winter's accumulation of snow.

Darius, on his invasion of Scythia about 508 B.C., commanded his fleet—which was manned principally by Ionian Greeks, together with some Aeolians and Greeks from the Hellespont—to sail up the Bosphorus and the Black Sea as far as the Danube, where they were to bridge the river for his army to cross. The fleet carried out these orders, sailing for two days up the Danube from one of its five mouths until they came to the place where the main stream divided. Here they built a bridge, presumably of boats, as Xerxes' engineers did for his crossing of the Hellespont.

After Darius with his army had marched up through Thrace and crossed the bridge, his first intention was to break it down so that the Ionians and others who had built it should be able to accompany him and his army on the march north. He was persuaded by Coes, the commander of the contingent from Mitylene, to leave the bridge intact so that the army would have a safe route back again. Coes said he was not looking for an excuse to stay behind guarding the bridge, since he would himself in any case accompany the army, and he was not afraid of being defeated in battle by the Scythians; what he was afraid of was that the army might not be able to find them. Darius agreed that there was something to be said for this point of view, and gave the Ionians a leather thong with sixty knots tied in it, telling them to untie one knot every day. They were to guard the bridge until all the knots were gone, and on that day they had his permission to sail for home.

After the Scythians' elusiveness, combined with their scorched-earth policy, had forced Darius to turn back, the Scythians sent deputations to the rulers of the Greek cities of the Hellespont and the Propontis, and of Ionia, asking them to destroy the bridge across the Danube so that Darius's retreat would be cut off. The Greek rulers met in conclave to discuss this proposition. Those present at the meeting included the despots of Abydos, Lampsacus, Parium (on the Propontis east of Lampsacus), Proconnesus, Cyzicus and Byzantium: and, from Ionia, the despots of Chios, Samos, Phocaea and Miletus, and of Cyme in Lydia.

Miltiades, tyrant of the Chersonese, advised not only the destruction of the bridge but also the sending of an expedition to liberate the Greek cities of Ionia. The opposing view was held by Histaeus of Miletus, who pointed out that everyone present at the meeting owed his position as head of state to the Persians. If Darius fell, they would fall with him, since every Greek state, once liberated, would reject despotic rule and choose freedom.

The argument of Histaeus convinced everyone at the meeting except Miltiades, who went ahead with his own plan to bring Lemnos and Imbros under the rule of Attica, having expelled the Pelasgians. As a result of this anti-Persian activity he had to flee from his despotate of the Chersonese when Darius's Phoenician fleet came along, after the suppression of the Ionian revolt.

Miltiades appears from this account of his activities in the light of a fervent Greek patriot, but his motives were—as is not uncommon— mixed. So, after playing his part in the defeat of the Persians at Marathon, he asked for seventy ships to lead against the Persians, and was granted them; but he used them to attack the island of Paros in pursuance of a private grudge. For this he was later impeached by Xanthippus, and died in prison of a wound on the leg acquired while trying to force an entry into a sacred enclosure during his attack on Paros. His son Cimon, who later commanded the Athenian fleet in various successful attacks on the Persians, appears as a purer patriot, but then he was not, like Miltiades, handicapped by having been born a hereditary tyrant.

Having seen as much as he could of the region around the mouths of the Danube, Herodotus sailed northwards from Istria towards his principal objective, the Greek city of Olbia at the mouth of the Bug (which he calls the Hypanis). The coast, as he remarks, sweeps round in a great bend where Scythia begins, north of the Danube. The mouth of the Dniester (the Tyras) was passed on the left; here there was a settlement of Greeks who called themselves Tyritae.

Beyond the mouth of the Dniester was the site of the modern city

of Odessa. Here the coastline turns sharply as the northernmost limit
of the Black Sea is reached, and runs eastwards to the place where the
great peninsula of the Crimea stands out from the land. Less than half-
way along this west–east stretch of coast is the great inlet into which
the rivers Bug and Dnieper flow. The city of Olbia lay on the shores
of this inlet, near the mouth of the Bug. Olbia was a Milesian colony
and the most important Greek city on the northern coasts of the
Black Sea. For Herodotus it was the natural centre from which he
could most conveniently inform himself about Scythia and the
Scythians. Some of that information was given him by a Greek called
Tymnes, the "agent" of Ariapithes, who was the son and successor
of Idanthyrsus, the king of the Scythians who fought against the
Persian invaders in 512 B.C.

He certainly travelled in the regions surrounding Olbia, but he
gives few details of where he went or what places he visited. His most
extensive journey inland appears to have been one he made up the
Dnieper, presumably in a Greek trading vessel, and he mentions this
only in an aside when speculating on the population of Scythia. He
visited a place called Exampaeus, west of the Dnieper and between it
and the Bug; which must have been somewhere in the region of
Cherkassy, south-east of Kiev. Around here a salt spring joined the
Bug, making its waters extremely salt for the rest of its course—a
four days' journey—towards the sea. The name "Exampaeus" meant,
in the Scythian language, "Sacred Ways". Here he was shown a
bronze bowl, six times as big as the one set up by Pausanias on the
headland where the Bosphorus opens out into the Black Sea. Its walls
were about four inches thick, and it could hold five thousand gallons.
The people of the district told him that one of the Scythian kings,
wishing to know the number of his subjects, had commanded every
man on pain of death to bring him a single arrowhead. In this way he
accumulated an immense pile of bronze arrowheads, and in order to
turn them into a permanent record he had them melted down into
this immense bowl.

Herodotus was no pioneer, forcing his way into unknown country
where the foot of Greek had never trod. He went where Greek
merchants already could and did go; but where they did and could go,
he was ready to go too. No one else in his time had the same unusual
impulse, or the ability to follow it.

Of the climate of Scythia, he says that the whole region suffered
from very severe winters. These lasted for eight months of the year,
and the cold during those months was so intense that the ground
froze as hard as iron. Even to make it muddy, water would not serve;
fire was needed. The Kerch Strait froze over, so that the Scythians

crossed it on waggons to attack the Sindian people of the Kuban. Even in the remaining four months of the year the weather was cold, and whereas no rain at all fell in the winter, when it would naturally be expected, in the summer it never stopped. Thunderstorms also occurred almost entirely in the summer, a winter thunderstorm being looked on as a rare phenomenon.

Horses stood the cold of winter well, but Herodotus was informed that mules and donkeys could not endure it at all. He thought that the bitter cold might also account for the cattle growing no horns, in contrast to their rapid growth in hot climates.

The rivers of Scythia were one of its most remarkable features, being larger and more numerous than anywhere else in the world. Herodotus reckoned there were eight major rivers, starting with the westernmost of them, the Danube. Next was the Dniester (the Tyras), which flowed southwards from a large lake and formed the boundary between the Scythians and the country of the Neuri. Then there was the Bug (the Hypanis), which also rose in a great lake round whose banks, he was told, white horses grazed. The water of the Bug was fresh for five days' sail downstream, but was then rendered brackish by the salt stream in the neighbourhood of Exampaeus; this was also the country of the people called Alazones. The Dniester and the Bug, as Herodotus accurately observes, drew near together in the country of the Alazones, in the upper parts of their courses, but diverged after leaving that country, so that a wide stretch of land lay between them.

The fourth river, the Dnieper or Borysthenes, Herodotus describes as the second largest of the rivers of Scythia after the Danube, and the most valuable and productive of any river in the world except the Nile. It provided the best and richest pasture, the finest and most abundant fish, and the purest drinking water; crops of any kind flourished in its basin. About the source and the upper course of the river he could discover no information; it entered the country of the agricultural Scythians from an uninhabited country at a place called Gerrhus, forty days' voyage up the river from its mouth, and for the first seven days its course lay through their territory.

In Herodotus's day the Dnieper and the Bug joined some short distance before reaching the sea. The point between them, where they joined, was called Cape Hippolaus, and there was a temple of Demeter, the goddess of agriculture, on it. The city of Olbia was situated on the other side of the Bug from the temple of Demeter.

The next river is a mere tributary, the Panticapes, which flows through Hylaea—the Woodland—southwards to join the Dnieper, the country between the Panticapes and Dnieper being that of the agricultural Scythians.

The sixth river, the Hypacyris, is one which flows—from a lake, like so many of them—through the country of the nomadic Scythians and reaches the sea near Carcinitis, leaving Hylaea and the place called Achilles' Racecourse on the right. The Hypacyris is difficult to identify. Carcinitis was situated somewhere near the corner of the Black Sea where the Crimea stands out to the south, and there is no river of any size that enters the Black Sea between here and the Dnieper. Achilles' Racecourse, whatever it was, has left no trace. The next river is the Gerrhus, which is said to "split off" from the Dnieper far to the north, in the place also called Gerrhus, where the Dnieper enters Scythian territory. It forms the boundary between the nomadic and the royal Scythians and runs finally into the Hypacyris.

Several rivers of no great importance run into the Sea of Azov east of the Crimea, and the Hypacyris and the Gerrhus might be assumed to be two of these, which Herodotus's informants had led him to believe were further west, but for one strange circumstance: his eighth river is the Don, and no mention is made of the Donetz, which lies between the Don and the Dnieper. One inescapable conclusion is that Herodotus never visited either, since what he has seen for himself he records accurately, but what he records from hearsay is distinctly less reliable. The other conclusion, a more tentative one, is that if his informants told him that there were two major rivers between the Dnieper and the Don, they are most likely to have been the Donetz, which flows into the Don about sixty miles above Rostov, and its major tributary the Oskol, though neither of these corresponds in the slightest to what Herodotus's informants told him about the Hypacyris and the Gerrhus.

Of the eighth river of Scythia there is no doubt It is the Don, the Tanais, which we are told rises, inevitably, in a large lake, far up into the interior, and, after dividing the territory of the royal Scythians from that of the Sarmatians, flows into the Sea of Azov. The grass growing in the region causes bile in cattle, as can be seen when the cattle are cut open; and, as a last contribution to the confusion, we are told that the Don is joined by another river, the Hyrgis, about which nothing more is said.

It is true that the Don is joined by many tributaries, some of them major rivers, such as the Ilovlya, the Medveditsa, and the Khoper, but the suspicion inevitably arises that the Hyrgis is most likely to have been the Donetz; in which case, where are the Hypacyris and the Gerrhus?

It is fortunate that these uncertainties do not cloud the general picture, which is clear enough. The five major rivers, the Danube, Dniester, Bug, Dnieper and Don, delineate satisfactorily in themselves

Herodotus's Journey to the North and the North East

Scythian human-headed monster from a felt appliqué
wall-hanging at a tomb in Pazyryk (c. 500 B.C.)

Kerch, the ancient city of Panticapaeum at the entrance to the Sea of Azov, was visited by Herodotus on his eastward journey from Olbia to Scythia, the Baltic and Thessaly.

the major divisions of Scythia as Herodotus describes it, and the elusiveness of the three minor ones does not invalidate the general picture.

For the people, Herodotus shows a modified lack of enthusiasm. Round the Black Sea, he said, there were to be found the most uncivilized nations on earth, lacking all the arts of civilized life. The only exception was the Scythians. He did not admire them greatly, but he did not think they were among the least civilized peoples on earth. And it had to be confessed that they managed one thing better than any other nation, and that was the most important of all: namely, their own self-preservation. Their way of life was such that no one who invaded their country could escape destruction, and if they wished to avoid battle with the invader there was no way in which he could come to grips with them. They had no fortified towns, but lived in waggons in which they could go where they pleased; every man was accustomed to fighting on horseback with bows and arrows; they did not depend on agriculture for their living but on their cattle. Because of this the invader not only could not conquer them, he could not even make contact with them.

This way of life was made possible for them by the nature of the country in which they lived, a fertile plain watered by numerous rivers and providing superb pasture.

They had a theory of their own to account for their origin. Herodotus says they claimed to be the youngest of all nations. The first man to live in Scythia, which was previously uninhabited, was a certain Targitaus, son of Zeus and a daughter of the river Dnieper. The Greeks of Pontus had a different story. They held that the Scythians were descended from Scythes, a son of Heracles. Heracles had come there—for what reason Herodotus does not say—with the oxen of Geryas from the far-away island of Erythea near Gades, or Cadiz. Having got to Scythia, he found it so bitterly cold that he went to sleep under his lion's skin. On waking, he perceived a creature half woman, half viper, who bore Scythes and other sons to him. Such a legend arouses improper doubts as to the wisdom of one's forefathers, and Herodotus himself says he does not believe the first one. Fortunately there is a third account, which stated that the original inhabitants of Scythia were Cimmerians, and that the Scythians then dwelt further east. When the Massagetae attacked them they moved westwards, being a nomadic people, and fell on the Cimmerians, some of whom fled, while the others were slain and buried in one enormous tomb by the river Hyras. Herodotus considers this story to be the most probable of the three, and mentions as supporting evidence that there were still traces left of the Cimmerians, such as the Cimmerian

Bosphorus—the name then given to the present Kerch Strait, by which the Sea of Azov is joined to the Black Sea—and Cimmeria, which was the region adjacent to it where the Cimmerians once lived.

This account is indeed astonishingly accurate. The Scythians were in fact an Indo-European people, related to both Greeks and Persians, and speaking a language related to both Greek and Persian, who migrated from central Asia to southern Russia in the eighth and seventh centuries B.C. The impetus for their movement came from far away on the borders of China. A group of nomadic tribes there called by the Chinese the Hiung-nu—possibly the ancestors of, and certainly related to, the Huns who invaded Europe twelve centuries later—were troubling the Chinese by incursions across their borders in the reign of the emperor Hsüan Wang, who reigned from 827 to 781 B.C. The emperor ordered a series of military operations against them, as a result of which they fell back from the Chinese frontiers westwards, setting up a general westward movement of the Asian nomadic tribes that finally dislodged the Massagetae from their grazing-grounds north of the Amu Darya, the Oxus. The Massagetae began to press on the Scythians west of them, and the Scythians, possibly troubled in addition by a drought at this period causing a general shortage of grazing, moved west too, to attack the Cimmerians in their lands north of the Caucasus and of the Black Sea.

As for the Cimmerians, some of them were slain, and the rest fled, as related by the account which Herodotus heard. The Scythians pursued the fleeing ones across Urartu, the land of Mount Ararat in what is now eastern Turkey, and westwards into Phrygia and Lydia, where they were finally wiped out. The first impact of the Scythians on recorded history is much as Herodotus describes it: their sudden appearance on the Persian border, their irruption into that region, culminating in their immense sweep southwards to the borders of Assyria. They established their rule in western Persia as far as the Halys; in 625 B.C. they invaded Syria and Judaea. They reached the borders of Egypt, but were prevented from invading that country by the wisdom, or weakness—or both—of the Pharaoh Psamtik I, who ruled from 663 to 610 B.C. and bought the Scythians off with bribes; an example of a successful payment of Danegeld that should not be entirely forgotten in condemning the numerous unsuccessful ones.

Their incursion, as sudden and as startling as that of the Huns hundreds of years later, was nearly as brief. They ruled western Persia in fact for twenty-eight years, at the end of which time the Medes ejected them, and they retired to their northern fastnesses. They dealt severely with the Persian invader, as Herodotus describes; but they did not again disturb on any large scale the peace of the people beyond their borders, though some Pontic cities had to pay tribute to them. The memory they left behind in Palestine caused the Hebrews to remember them in their scriptures as the people of Gog and Magog.

Herodotus identifies several tribes or divisions of the Scythian people. West of the Bug, inland from Olbia, was a tribe called the Callipidae, and east of them, between the Bug and the Dnieper, to the east, were the Alazones. Both, as far as their language and ways of life were concerned, were Scythians, but they differed from true Scythians in that they were not nomadic, but agrarian, growing grain, onions, leeks, lentils and millet. North of them, too, there were tribes engaged in agriculture, until the borders of Scythia were reached.

East of the Dnieper, starting inland from the coast, there was the wooded region called the Hylaea, and northwards of this more of the agricultural Scythians, those nearer Olbia being known to other Scythians as Olbiopolites, though the Greeks called them Borysthenites, people of the Dnieper. The agricultural Scythians extended eastwards from the Dnieper as far as its tributary the Panticapes, about three days' journey, and beyond the Panticapes began the country of the nomadic Scythians, who followed the way of life of their Asian ancestors and had not yet started to settle the land and grow crops.

Herodotus estimates that the land of the agricultural Scythians extended northwards up the Bug as far as a boat could sail in eleven days.

The nomadic Scythians, east of the Panticapes, occupied the country for fourteen days' journey eastwards to the mysterious river Gerrhus; and eastwards of this lay the people whom Herodotus calls the royal Scythians, in the country of the Kings. These were the most numerous and warlike of the Scythians and the other tribes were subservient to them. Their country extended southwards into the Crimea as far as the mountainous south of the peninsula, where the untamed Tauri lived, and inland it ran eastwards as far as the Don; though along the shores of the Sea of Azov Herodotus says it extended only as far as the Greek trading post of Cremni.

The whole of their country, except for the Hylaea, was bare and treeless.

Of the characteristics of the Scythians noted by Herodotus, an outstanding one was their xenophobia. This is of course a widespread characteristic of most peoples in most ages, and the Scythians appear to have possessed it to about the normal extent, so that they despised the Greeks, for example, just about as much as the Greeks despised them, not appreciably more or noticeably less. The main body of

Scythian opinion considered Greek ways to be both ludicrous and undesirable. Some royal Scythians thought otherwise, and the harsh treatment meted out to them by their countrymen illustrates the repulsion which Greek customs inspired in Scythians generally.

Anarcharsis, a Scythian whom Herodotus considered to have been the most civilized man that the nation had produced, travelled widely in the Greek world. Having observed the people of Cyzicus celebrating a festival in honour of the Mother of the Gods, he decided he would do the same when he got home. He was seen in a wood at night with the ritual images fastened to his clothing and a drum in his hand. The person who saw him indulging in these outlandish rites reported the matter to the king, who came in person with his bow and arrow and shot Anarcharsis dead. A king of Scythia, Scylas, was attracted by the mysteries of Dionysus, and, having been initiated into the cult, was seen by his own people indulging in Bacchic orgies. The Scythians, thinking it shameful to imagine that there could be such a thing as a god who drove people out of their wits, rose in rebellion. Scylas ran away to Thrace but was handed back by the Thracians to his own people, who beheaded him.

Such was Scythian xenophobia, and Herodotus might easily have seen it as excessive, but it is true to say that if Herodotus had been seen by his compatriots in Samos or Halicarnassus chopping off the head of his enemy and using it as a drinking-cup, there would have been some manifestation of public disesteem. The wise man, whether or not he admires the customs he finds abroad, does not expect them to find instant acceptance in his own country.

The principal object of worship of the Scythians was the deity they called Tabiti, which Herodotus regarded as the equivalent of the Greek Hestia, the virgin goddess of the hearth, later called by the Romans Vesta. Other gods were Papaeus, similar to Zeus, the father of the gods; Api, or Earth, whom the Scythians believed to be the wife of Papaeus; Oetosyrus, or Apollo, god of poetry and song, healing, prophecy, plague, the protection of cattle and crops, and other matters, closely identified by Herodotus's time with the sun; Argimpasa, identified with Aphrodite, goddess of love and beauty; and the god of war, whose Scythian name is not divulged, but whose Greek equivalent was Ares. Heracles, the Greek hero, son of Zeus and Alcmene, was also worshipped; and the royal Scythians alone worshipped Thagimasadas, or Poseidon, the sea-god.

The Scythians did not make statues, set up altars or build temples to any god except Ares. The mode of worship was by sacrifice, normally of an animal. The animal's forefeet were tied together; the rope binding them was pulled so that the animal fell down, while at the same time the person conducting the sacrifice called on the appropriate god; a noose was then slipped round the animal's neck, a short stick was pushed through the noose, and the stick was twisted until the animal was strangled to death. There was no libation of wine, or burning of incense, nor was any part of the animal burned in a fire, as was the Greek custom. The victim was skinned and the flesh boiled in a cauldron. Owing to the shortage of wood in Scythia it was often the practice to strip the flesh from the bones, and use the bones to feed the fire below the cauldron; Herodotus remarks that they burned well. If no cauldron was available the flesh was put with water into the animal's stomach, and the whole was boiled over the fire. When the meat was cooked a portion of it was thrown down on the ground as a sacrifice to the god, the rest being eaten by the worshippers. Horses were the animals most commonly sacrificed. Cattle were sacrificed less often, and pigs never, since these animals were not bred in Scythia at all. They were unsuited to a nomadic life, and preferred wooded country.

The temples to Ares took a peculiar form, consisting of enormous piles of brushwood, three furlongs square, the top being levelled off to form a platform. One side was made less steep than the other three, to provide access. Every year a hundred and fifty waggon-loads of brushwood were added to the pile to make up for the settling caused by the rains. An ancient iron sword was planted upright on top of the pile, to serve as the image of Ares. There was one of these brushwood-temples or mounds at the chief seat of government of every district. Annual sacrifices of horses and other cattle were made to the sword, more victims being sacrificed to Ares than to any of the other gods.

Prisoners of war were also sacrificed to Ares. One man was chosen out of every hundred prisoners; wine was poured over his head and his throat was cut over a bowl. The bowl was carried to the top of the mound and the blood poured over the sword. The right hands and right arms of the victims were cut off from the bodies at the foot of the pile, thrown up in the air and allowed to lie where they fell.

In war, it was customary for every man to drink the blood of the first man he killed in battle. The heads of all enemies killed were taken to be shown to the king. Warriors, who were all free Scythian tribesmen, were fed and clothed but were paid no wage. If a man brought a head of a foeman he was given his share of the loot, otherwise he received nothing.

The skin was stripped off the heads by making a circular cut above the ears and peeling it from the skull. The skin was scraped clean of flesh with an ox-rib, and when it was clean it was worked with the fingers until it was supple. It was then hung from the bridle of its owner's horse, along with other similar skins, as a sign of prowess. Sometimes several of these skins would be sewn together to make a kind of cloak. The skin from other parts of the enemy's body might also be used in other ways, that of the hands and arms being used to cover quivers.

The scalped skulls of the most despised or hated enemies were sawn off at the eyebrows and used, after cleaning out the contents, as drinking-vessels. Wealthier Scythians would gild the inside of these drinking-skulls. If a man quarrelled with his kinsman and defeated him in single combat before the king, he might deal with his skull in the same way. When entertaining important visitors a man would pass his collection of skulls round and tell the stories of how he acquired them. The governor of every district gave a wine-feast each year, and those who had killed their enemies in battle were allowed to drink from the wine-bowl, those who had killed the greatest numbers being allowed to fill two cups at once; but those who had killed no enemies were barred from the feast, this being the greatest disgrace they could suffer.

There were many soothsayers in Scythia. Their method of working suggests that their lore was based, if not on the *I Ching* itself—that ancient Chinese work of divination was already more than half a millennium old—then on some similar and perhaps related scheme learned during the Scythians' residence in central Asia. As Herodotus describes it, bundles of willow-rods were laid on the ground, untied and laid out singly, the prophecy being then pronounced while the rods were being collected again and tied into bundles. This was the normal method, but the rival sect of magicians or priests Herodotus calls Enarees used a different technique; they would cut a piece of the inner bark of the lime-tree into pieces and twist and untwist them round their fingers while they made their prophecies.

When the king fell ill three of the most reputable soothsayers were sent for to carry out the customary divination by the use of willow-rods. The usual conclusion was that some man had sworn by the king's hearth, this being the oath used for the most solemn declarations, but had sworn falsely. The accused man was then brought into the king's presence and charged with his offence by the soothsayers. On his denial of the offence the king would send for more soothsayers, six instead of the original three, and command them to carry out a divination in their turn. If they agreed that the defendant was guilty, he would immediately be beheaded and his property divided among the original three soothsayers; a custom which suggests that wealthy Scythians must have been extremely vulnerable to soothsayers, unless they made large and frequent contributions to the fraternity to keep on the right side of them.

If, however, the new soothsayers found the accused man not guilty, more soothsayers would be brought in, and if necessary more again. If in the end the majority of the soothsayers declared the accused man to be innocent, the law demanded that the original three soothsayers should be executed. This was done by filling a cart with sticks and harnessing oxen to it. The soothsayers, gagged and bound, were thrust down among the sticks, which were then set on fire, and the oxen scared so that they set off at a run. Sometimes the oxen would be burned to death as well as the soothsayers, but sometimes the pole of the cart would be burned through before the fire reached the sooth-sayers, so that they escaped.

When any criminal was executed his sons were also put to death, but the females of the family were not harmed.

The Enarees, described by Herodotus as "a class of effeminate persons", were soothsayers or magicians who seem to be distinguished by him from the normal run of soothsayers by their use of a different method of divination. They were said to speak in high-pitched voices and dress as women. According to the Scythians, certain of their number robbed the temple of the Great Goddess at Ashkelon, during the Scythians' irruption into Syria, and the goddess punished them for this offence by visiting them with the "female disease", from which their descendants still suffered. The Enarees remain a rather mysterious feature of Scythian life, and whether the visitation of the "female disease" turned them into homosexuals, heterosexual transvestites, eunuchs, sufferers from venereal disease, or something else, remains far from clear.

The taking of oaths was performed among the Scythians by drawing blood from both parties to the oath by pricking the arm with a sharp point or cutting it with a dagger, and allowing the blood to drip into an earthenware bowl full of wine. Some weapons—a sword, a battle-axe or bill, a javelin and a few arrows—were dipped into the wine, and prayers were said; the two parties to the oath and their chief supporters then drank the mingled wine and blood.

When a king died, his body was preserved by slitting it open, clearing out the contents, and filling it with a mixture which included various aromatic herbs, galingale, parsley-seed and aniseed. The body was sewn up again and coated with wax and then carried on a waggon in procession among the various tribes. Those among whom it passed mutilated themselves in various ways, by slitting their ears, shaving their heads, cutting their arms, foreheads and noses or trans-piercing their left hands with arrows. The tribe joined the procession as it passed among them and followed the body until, having been taken to every district of Scythia, it reached the burial-place of the Scythian kings in the remote north of the country, where the Gerrhus enters it.

The body was then laid on a mattress on the floor of an immense square pit dug ready to receive it. Spears were fixed in the ground around it to support a roof of withies laid on wooden poles. Various members of the king's household—his butler, his groom, his cook, his steward, his chamberlain and one of his concubines—were strangled and laid in the tomb around him, along with horses, gold cups and other miscellaneous treasures. The tomb was then filled in and an immense mound of earth raised over it.

A year after the king's death, another ceremony took place. Fifty of the king's most faithful servants were strangled, and their bodies gutted, stuffed with straw and sewn up again. (These were native Scythians, since the king had no foreign-born slaves.) Fifty of his finest horses were slaughtered, gutted and stuffed in a similar manner. The horses were then mounted upright by driving poles through them from front to rear and supporting these on wheels sawn in half and fixed in pairs, rim down, to stakes driven into the ground, two stakes to each half-wheel. The horses' legs were left dangling on either side. The bodies of the servants were then treated in a similar way, poles being driven up through them and fitted into sockets in the poles supporting the horses. In this way the king's tomb was surrounded with a bodyguard of fifty servants on horseback.

When an ordinary Scythian died his relations took the body round in a cart to visit friends. These would entertain the guests with a meal, food being served to the corpse along with the others. After this round of visits had gone on for forty days, the body was buried.

After the burial the relations went through a process of ritual cleansing, washing their heads with soap and their bodies in a vapour-bath. Herodotus describes this vapour-bath in some detail. A small tent was erected by stretching woollen cloths round three tent-poles tied together at the top. Inside the tent the person taking the bath would place a dish of red-hot stones, then, crawling into the tent, throw hemp-seed on to the stones. The vapour given off was found so delectable by the Scythians that they used to howl with pleasure while taking one of these baths.

The details of the process are accurately described, but Herodotus here has misinterpreted the purpose. The Scythians were in the habit of inhaling the fumes of roasting hempseeds in the manner described, but they did it not for ritual purification but for pleasure; it was the Scythian equivalent of pot-smoking or glue-sniffing. In the frozen tombs excavated at Pazyryk small tents of leather or felt were found, with, below them, cauldrons filled with stones and hempseeds. They were left there, along with all the other goods and gear, for the use of the deceased, and the purpose of the hemp-tent was to give him the pleasure of inhaling hemp-fumes; to give him his kicks, in fact, in the after-life.

The Scythians, Herodotus remarks, never washed their bodies with water. The women would plaster themselves all over with a paste made of cedar-wood, cypress-wood and frankincense ground on a rough stone and mixed with water. When they had left this on for a day they would scrape it off, leaving their skins clean and sweet-smelling.

The Scythians had neighbours round their borders, in a great arc stretching from the Danube at one end to the Don at the other. On the northern banks of the Danube, westwards of Scythian territory— that is, in the western parts of modern Romania, and extending into Hungary—lived the Agathyrsi, who, Herodotus says, strongly resembled the Thracians in their manners and customs. They were a wealthy people, given to wearing gold ornaments, and shared their women among themselves, so that they could live like members of one enormous family, without jealousy or hatred.

To the north-west of the Scythians, that is, in the region of the present Slovakia and southern Poland, lived the Neuri, whose way of life resembled that of the Scythians. Herodotus tells a story of their being driven from their homeland in the generation before Darius, seventy or eighty years before his time, by an invasion of snakes from the uninhabited country to the north. They were forced by this incursion to move east to the lands of the Budini. Like many of Herodotus's hearsay stories of realms he never visited himself, this probably enshrines a folk-memory of some actual event in either a recent or a remote age, but it seems impossible now to determine what that event might have been.

In Scythia, and among the Greeks in Scythia, it was said that the Neuri were practised magicians, and that once a year every man of the Neuri turned himself into a wolf. Having been a wolf for a few days, he turned back into a man again. Herodotus says he personally does not believe this story, but his informants were prepared to swear it was true. Herodotus's scepticism was in advance of his age, since a belief in werewolves has lingered on in backward regions of Europe till the present century, and in the fifteenth century—nearly two thousand years after Herodotus's time—a council of theologians under the chairmanship of the Emperor Sigismund ruled that there were indeed werewolves, and they were much to be abhorred.

Beyond the Neuri the country was uninhabited; but east of them, between the Neuri and the Melanchlaeni, lived the savage Andro-phagi. This was in the region of Kiev and the western Ukraine. Herodotus says the Androphagi were the only people in this part of the world to eat human flesh, though in saying so he appears to forget what he has said elsewhere of the Massagetae and their way of dealing with elderly relatives. They wore clothing like that of the Scythians, but they spoke a language of their own, and were nomad herdsmen who built no fixed dwellings. Beyond them, as with the Neuri, the country was an uninhabited wilderness.

Northwards of the royal Scythians, and eastwards of the Andro-phagi—in the region of the modern Kharkov—lived the Melanch-laeni, so called from the black cloaks they wore. They were, says Herodotus, apparently closely related to the Scythians, and except for these black cloaks resembled them in all respects. North of them lay an uninhabited wilderness with many lakes.

East of the Melanchlaeni, along the north-eastern borderlands of Scythia, lived the Budini. They occupied a large territory in the upper Don basin, and were a numerous and powerful people. Many of them had blue-grey eyes and red hair, and they had a language and culture of their own, but Herodotus gives few details of either except to say that they were a nomadic people of herdsmen, whose peculiar habit it was to eat lice.

There was in their territory, however, a town called Gelonus, built entirely of wood, with wooden houses and wooden temples and a wooden wall surrounding it, between three and four miles in length and in breadth. The temples were dedicated to the worship of Greek gods, and contained, like Greek temples, altars, statues and shrines, though all these were made of wood. A triennial festival was held there in honour of Dionysus. The people of the town, the Geloni, were quite different from the Budini, being descended from Greeks who had been driven out of some coastal settlement and had settled inland, among the alien people. Their language was half Scythian and half Greek, and they lived a quite different life from the pastoral Budini, since they tilled the soil, ate grain and cultivated gardens. Their appearance and their complexions were also quite different from those of the Budini among whom they dwelt.

Herodotus emphasizes strongly the fact that the Geloni and Budini were quite different people, although the local Greeks, his informants, tended to lump them all together under the name of Geloni. He had a persistent interest, unique in his own time and rare for many centuries to come, in peoples other than his own; and it is rather agreeable to catch a glimpse of him here, arguing with his fellow-Greeks, the colonists of Olbia or Panticapes, that the natives up in Gelonus, the illiterate nomads who herded their cattle about in the bush beyond the cultivated land, were not merely an inconsiderable feature of the background, like the birds and the bushes, but people, like the colonists themselves. It is doubtful, though, whether this eccentricity earned him much esteem. An advantaged social group living in contact with a disadvantaged one usually both accounts for and justifies its advantages by assuming itself to be inherently superior to an extent that virtually makes it out to be a different species.

North-east of the Budini, whose land was largely bare of trees, was a wooded region inhabited by peoples called Thyssagetae and Iyrcae, who lived by hunting. And eastwards of these was a tribe of Scythians who had left their own country because of some quarrel with the royal Scythians, and lived in exile there. Hereabouts the flat plains of rich soil that were characteristic of Scythia began to give way to a more rugged and stony plain, and this rose gradually to the foothills of a mountain range. In these foothills lived a tribe of people who were completely bald, both men and women, with snub noses and long chins. The bald people lived on the fruit of a certain tree called ponticum, the ripe fruit being strained through cloths and the liquid lapped up with the tongue, or mixed with milk for drinking. Each man lived under his own ponticum-tree, guarding it against the winter cold by wrapping bands of white felt round its trunk, and taking them off again in the summer.

These bald men were called Argippaei. They had no weapons, but nobody attacked them, and they were called in to settle quarrels among their neighbours. Anybody who took refuge among them was allowed to live there in peace. They seemed, as Herodotus says, to be guarded by a kind of sanctity.

It is noticeable, and natural, that the further away a country is, the odder its people become. The neighbours across the border merely wear black cloaks or eat lice; but beyond them are the peaceful bald men with their swaddled ponticum-trees, and beyond these again, still going more or less north and east, was an impassable range of mountains inhabited by men with goats' feet, and beyond these was a nation of men who slept for six months of the year. Herodotus found it impossible to believe in either of these last two stories.

The Scythians' last immediate neighbours, across the Don to the east, and east, too, of the Sea of Azov as far as the Caspian, were the Sauromatae. Herodotus has a story that a band of Amazons, after being defeated in battle and captured by a band of Greeks in their country near the river Thermodon, were taken away by them on their three ships, but overcame their captors. Being unable to handle the ships, they had been blown northwards across the Black Sea to the Sea of Azov. Here they terrified and looted the country for a time until they fell to the wiles of some young Scythian warriors, who gradually overcame their suspicions, and finally took them as wives.

The young Scythians wanted their wives to travel home with them, but they refused, saying that they and the Scythian women could never live together, since their ways differed too much. They were horsewomen and could use the bow and the spear, but knew nothing of women's work; whereas the Scythian women stayed at home in their waggons and never went out to hunt or to make war. It would be better, they said, if the young men went back to their parents to collect any inheritance due to them and returned to live with the Amazons a life that suited both of them. The young men agreed, as they did to the Amazons' further suggestion that, since they had done a certain amount of damage by raiding when they first came into the country, it would be better if they all went off and lived somewhere else, beyond the river Don. They all accordingly crossed the Don and, having travelled for three days east and three days north, settled down in the country where they were still living. There the Amazons were able to keep to their old ways, and the women of the Sauromatae still did so, hunting and making war either with or without the men, and wearing the same sort of clothes as them. Herodotus says the Sauromatae spoke a form of Scythian corrupted by the fact that the Amazons never learned to speak it properly. It was the law among them that a girl should not marry until she had killed an enemy in battle, and some of their women remained unmarried for life because they had been unable to do so.

The lands of the Sauromatae stretched as far as the Caspian, which, as Herodotus's informants correctly told him, was a sea in itself, not connected with any other sea. In this it differed from the Mediterranean, which was joined through the Pillars of Hercules— the Straits of Gibraltar—to the Atlantic, which in its turn was joined to the Indian Ocean, so that all these were really parts of one sea. The Caspian was reckoned to be fifteen days' rowing in length, and eight in breadth. On its west rose the Caucasus, thought to be the longest and highest of mountain ranges, while on its east was an immense stretch of flat country over which the eye could wander until it was lost in the distance.

Most of this vast plain was occupied by the Massagetae, who were said to resemble the Scythians in their costume and way of life. In war, though, they fought on foot as well as on horseback, the dismounted warriors including archers, spearmen, and men wielding the bill, or long-handled axe. The only metals known to them were gold, which they used for helmets, belts and girdles, besides bridles, bits and cheek-pieces for horses, and bronze, which was used for spearheads, arrowheads, bills and breastplates for horses. They had no silver or iron, and knew nothing of them.

Every man of the Massagetae had a wife, but all wives were used promiscuously; Herodotus remarks that the Greeks believed this to be a Scythian custom, but in fact it was the Massagetae who practised it. If a man wanted any particular woman all he had to do was to hang up his quiver in front of the waggon where she was living, and go in and enjoy her without fear of interruption. They had a way of deciding when it was time for a man to die and ensuring that he did so: when he reached a great age, his relations all gave a great party and sacrificed the man along with the cattle. His flesh was boiled and eaten by the guests along with the rest. They considered this to be the best way of all to die, and those who did not live long enough to be sacrificed were thought to be unlucky.

The Massagetae did not practise agriculture at all, but lived on meat and fish, of which they found abundant supplies in the principal river of their country. The river referred to may have been the Jaxartes or Syr Darya, east of the Aral Sea, though much that Herodotus says about it suggests the Volga. They were milk-drinkers, and worshipped no god but the sun, to whom they sacrificed horses, the idea being to sacrifice the swiftest of animals to the swiftest of the gods.

North of the Massagetae, and east of the Argippaei, lay the country of the Issedones, of whom Herodotus could learn little except that when a man died among them his relations brought sheep to the house to be sacrificed. The bodies of the sheep and the man were sliced up and their meat eaten together as a funeral feast. This seems to link them with the Massagetae; but another custom of their own was to empty the dead man's head of its contents, shave it and gild it and offer sacrifices to it, as an object of worship.

For more information about the Issedones and their neighbours further to the north still, Herodotus cites Aristeas, a poet who lived some time earlier than Herodotus, though whether a hundred years or four hundred years earlier is uncertain. Aristeas was a native of Proconnesus who claimed in his epic poem, *The Arimaspea*, that in a vision—inspired by Phoebus, as he puts it—he travelled northwards from the land of the Scythians to that of the Issedones. These people told him that further north still lay the land of the one-eyed Arimaspeans, and beyond them a country where the griffins guarded the gold. Further north still were the Hyperboreans, whose land ended at the sea. In some earlier age, they said, the Arimaspeans had attacked the

Issedones, expelling them from the country in which they then lived, whereon the Issedones had attacked the Scythians and the Scythians the Cimmerians.

Herodotus adds little to this in the way of comment except to remark that if there are Hyperboreans—people living beyond Boreas, the north wind, as the name implies—there must also be Hypernotians, people living beyond the south wind Notus, or Auster. However it is interesting to note that even in this mythic account of the north, along perhaps with less easily identifiable fragments of facts in disguise, there is a quite clear picture of the process of one people pushing another further on by which the Scythians did in fact reach their contemporary homeland: the domino theory, looming darkly in the folk-memory more or less as it actually occurred, if swung round a little northwards.

If Herodotus obtained little information about the Hyperboreans while he was in Scythia, something was added to it by the people of Delos in the Cyclades, since the Hyperboreans were in the habit of sending certain sacred offerings to the shrine there, the major centre of the worship of Apollo. In Herodotus's day these were passed from hand to hand from one people to another—a kind of voluntary postal service—by a singularly complicated route through Scythia, Thrace, Macedonia, Dodona in Epirus, the gulf of Malis, Euboea, Tenos in the Cyclades and thence to the great temple of Apollo on Delos. However, in an earlier time they were actually brought the whole way by Hyperborean girls. It was the tendency of the girls to die on the journey that led the Hyperboreans to resort to the device of wrapping the offerings in straw and handing them to the neighbouring nation across the border with the request that they should be passed on along their long route.

It appears therefore that at some more or less remote time Hyperboreans had actually been seen in the Aegean; but from what nation they in fact came remains a mystery. Only one glimpse remains of the Russian north, as Herodotus heard of it: the Scythians told him that it was impossible to travel through these regions to the north of their own country, since the air was so full of falling feathers it was impossible to see where one was going. Herodotus repeats the story, but adds that in his own opinion it arises merely from the frequency of snowstorms in those regions.

As for the east, beyond the Massagetae, Herodotus has no information except that Asia is inhabited as far as India, but that further east it is both uninhabited and entirely unknown.

Modern archaeological research shows that all the tribes described by Herodotus as neighbours of the Scythians were, in fact, Scythians themselves: including the Agathyrsi, the Neuri, the Melanchlaeni, the Budini, even the Androphagi. The Sauromatae, whom history knew later as the Sarmatians, were not exactly Scythians, but they were closely related to them. The dominant group, at least, was of the same Indo-European stock, with a similar language, though there may have been other tribal groups there, in the country between the Sea of Azov and the Caspian, who descended from peoples less recently arrived in the area and survived now, under the rule of the dominant Sarmatians, with a status in society ranging from association on more or less equal terms to near-serfdom. Those more closely akin, and existing in alliance with the Sarmatians rather than in subservience to them, included the Alani, of the Kuban valley north of the Caucasus, and the Roxolani of the Volga basin.

In the generations succeeding Herodotus's visit to Scythia the strength of the ruling group in Scythia, the royal Scythians north of the Crimea, was sapped by their conflicts with Philip of Macedonia. The Sarmatians, unaffected by this warfare, gradually moved westwards, forcing the Scythians from their homeland, and, in the course of several centuries, conquered and supplanted them; until by the second century A.D. what had been Scythia was known as Sarmatia.

There were other neighbours of the Scythians, on the south, who were no relations at all. These were the Tauri, who lived in the southern part of the Crimea, the Tauric Chersonese, and had lived in those regions long before the Scythians came and confined them to their mountainous refuge. Herodotus sailed along this coast when, after his stay in Olbia, he journeyed eastwards to the Sea of Azov. It was a dangerous voyage, since any seamen who happened to be cast up there, and in particular any Greeks, were seized and sacrificed by the Tauri to the Maiden Goddess. Herodotus was fully informed of the procedure awaiting him in case of shipwreck. The victim, after preliminary prayers had been said over him and libations poured, was hit over the head with a club. The body was then either pushed over the cliff or buried, and the head was stuck on a stake. The goddess to whom these sacrifices were made was very ancient, but she had become transformed to some extent by the influence of the Greeks in all these regions, and the Tauri themselves claimed that she was Agamemnon's daughter Iphigenia.

When the Greek fleet, being ready to sail against Troy, was detained by a calm in Aulis, the sage Calchas told Agamemnon that the goddess Artemis was angry with him because he had once killed one of her stags while out hunting. This was only one of the reasons given, and there were others, but the truth was that Artemis, like her brother Apollo, was notoriously pro-Trojan.

Artemis, Calchas said, could only be placated by the sacrifice of Agamemnon's daughter Iphigenia. Being persuaded that this was so, Agamemnon had Iphigenia brought to Chalcis, in Euboea, on the pretext of marrying her to Achilles. He was about to sacrifice her to Artemis, who had a temple there at Aulis, when Artemis carried her off in a cloud to Tauris, leaving a stag to be sacrificed in her place. In Tauris, Iphigenia became a priestess of Artemis; and it was while she was there that her brother Orestes came to carry off the statue of the goddess. He was caught in the act, and would have been sacrificed to her, but that in the nick of time Iphigenia recognized him and fled with him to Delphi.

The worship of Artemis, even in the elegantly dressed-up Greek version familiar to Herodotus, was a rough and dangerous business, and the Tauric version of Artemis was nearer to the original, a much less poetic and much more basic female. The Tauri were in no way reconciled to the two civilizations hemming them in, the Scythians with their romantic cloaks and gold ornaments to the north of them, or the Greeks whose cities and colonies sought a foothold on their hostile coastline. Other people, such as the Thracians, were still addicted to lopping off people's heads, as indeed was Richard Cœur de Lion sixteen hundred years later, when he rode about Syria taking off the heads of Saracens and hanging them in bunches from his saddle-bow; but the Tauri went further. When one of them defeated an enemy in battle he would lop off his head and stick it on a pole on top of his dwelling, to act as a guardian of the house and its inhabitants. Like the Thracians, too, they regarded the plunder of war as the only income fit for a gentleman; being, in this, not unlike Europeans of the nineteenth century, or even later.

Herodotus, avoiding shipwreck and its attendant decapitation, sailed on to the cities of Panticapaeum and Phanagoria, which were situated on opposite shores of the Cimmerian Bosphorus, or Strait of Kerch, the channel connecting the Sea of Azov with the Black Sea. Panticapaeum was founded by the Milesians in 541 B.C., and was a city of major importance, with an excellent harbour and a commanding situation. It was knocked about badly by the Huns in A.D. 375, but was still flourishing in the time of Justinian, who built new walls for it more than a thousand years after Herodotus's time. The Mongols ceded it to the Genoese in 1388, and the Turks to the Russians in 1771, and now it is called Kerch, a flourishing centre for ship repairing, railway engineering, fish canning and the digging out of iron ore and turning of it into steel; but there are still fragments of its ancient past to be seen there, burial mounds and catacombs and other relics of the Greek city of long ago.

A Greek hoplite, or heavy-armed infantryman. In the Athenian army hoplites were accompanied by attendants who looked after their baggage and carried their shields on the march. Herodotus gleaned and recorded massive information by befriending both the hoplites and their attendants about the battles they experienced, the lands they traversed and the customs and natures of the many peoples they encountered. Herodotus, the father of history, was also the first investigative journalist.

Opposite it, on the eastern side of the Straits, was Phanagoria, a Teian colony, with a temple of Aphrodite Apaturos, and a steadily increasing trade with the south-eastern coasts of the Black Sea, the cities of Pontus and Colchis.

Panticapaeum had been founded nearly eighty years at the time of Herodotus's visit to Scythia, and its traders were certainly familiar with all the coastlands of Lake Maeotis, the Sea of Azov. Greek agents and commercial depots were planted there, channels through which flowed the trade of Scythia with the Greek world. Up at the north-eastern corner of Lake Maeotis, the Don flowed into the sea, below where Rostov-on-Don now stands. The Don was a channel for merchandise, and for the penetration of Greek merchants inland, to the tribes who had furs and gold to exchange for Greek earthenware, trinkets, exotic oddments for the wives of chieftains. Up there a Greek could travel; and up there, it seems, Herodotus went, on his ultimate venture into the interior, since he speaks of the forts erected by Darius which were still to be seen there in his day, in that remote and little-visited region.

When Darius crossed the Danube, the Scythians asked all their neighbours to come to their aid, but only the Geloni, the Budini and the Sauromatae were willing to do so. The Agathyrsi, the Neuri, the Androphagi, the Melanchlaeni and the Tauri all declined, on the grounds that the Scythians were the original aggressors, which was true, the Scythians having in the time of Cyrus invaded Persia from the east of the Caspian. They would do nothing against the Persians, these tribesmen said, unless the Persians first attacked them.

It was this refusal of aid that led the Scythians to avoid pitched battle and retire in front of Darius's advance, blocking up all the wells and springs and trampling down the pasture. They split their army into two, and the Persians pursued one division eastwards through Scythia and across the Don, into the remote territory of the Budini and the Geloni. Here they burned the wooden city of Gelonus, which had been abandoned by its inhabitants. The Scythians went on retreating, and the Persians went on following, into an uninhabited region beyond the territory of the Budini. Here, on the banks of an unidentifiable river called the Oarus, Darius halted and had eight large forts built, approximately eight miles apart. These are the forts which Herodotus states were still to be seen in his day.

While Darius was building them, the Scythians continued to retreat, making a broad sweep to the northward and then westward, and finally returned to Scythia. Darius, having no news of them, left the forts half finished and turned back towards Scythia in search of them. When he reached Scythia he made contact with the other half of the

C

Scythian army, who retreated northwards into the country of the
Melanchlaeni, and thence to those of the Androphagi and the Neuri.
They made then—always pursued by the Persians—for the country
of the Agathyrsi, but the Agathyrsi were averse to the idea of being
invaded twice, first by Scythians and then by Persians, so they gathered
all their warriors on the frontier, prepared to defend it. The Scythians,
having no quarrel with them and plenty of room for manoeuvre,
turned southwards back to Scythia.

At this point Darius managed to send a messenger to the Scythians.
Why, he asked the Scythian king Idanthyrsus, did he keep on running
away? He really had only two alternatives: either to stand and fight,
or to send Darius earth and water as tokens of submission, and come
to a conference.

Idanthyrsus replied, saying he had never run away from any man,
and was not doing so now. He was living the sort of life he customarily lived, and intended to continue in this way. He acknowledged no
master, and would send Darius some presents in due course, but not
the ones he asked for.

After this exchange the Scythians stepped up their action a little,
sending out raiding parties to attack the Persians when they were
foraging for supplies. They also sent a force to negotiate with the
Ionians the breaking down of the bridge over the Danube, and initiated a series of cavalry attacks on the Persians, retreating again when
the Persian cavalry fell back on the infantry. The only difficulty they
encountered in this part of the campaign arose from the braying of
donkeys and the strange appearance of some unfamiliar animals,
mules, in the Persian army. Since neither animal was known in Scythia
the horses were startled by them, but this inconvenience did not cause
any major setback in the Scythian operations. At this time Idanthyrsus,
having allowed a decent delay to take place, sent Darius a present,
though not the earth and water asked for. It consisted of a bird, a frog,
five arrows and a mouse. Various interpretations were put forward by
eminent Persians in conclave, but Gobryas, who had helped Darius
to turn his predecessor off the throne and felt reasonably confident of
his own safety, said that in his opinion it meant that unless the Persians
could fly up into the air like birds, dig themselves holes in the ground
like mice or jump into the lake like frogs, all they had coming to them
was arrows.

Whether or not Darius agreed with this interpretation, it was at
this point that he decided to abandon the campaign, and set off one
night to march back to the Danube, leaving behind his sick and
wounded and the donkeys, whose braying would deceive the enemy
into thinking that the Persian army was still in position.

Herodotus, having viewed Darius's half-finished forts in the country of the Budini east of the Don—the ultimate limit of his travels in Scythia, as it was for Darius—returned to Panticapaeum on the Cimmerian Bosphorus. From there it would be natural to assume that he returned home, except that he makes it clear in his book, without any shadow of ambiguity, that he went to Colchis; and if he went to Colchis he can hardly have gone there on any occasion but this. In Panticapaeum he was much nearer to Colchis than he ever was again. The only other time he was within five hundred miles of it was when, on his journey to Babylon, he passed—presumably—through Myriandrus, a few miles south of Iskenderun at the extreme north-east corner of the Mediterranean.

Even if he had travelled the royal road to Susa, the Persian capital, from Sardis, in his later eastern travels, he would have been separated from Colchis by the whole mountainous width of Armenia. Xenophon and the Ten Thousand made a similar journey, but it was touch and go even for an army led by a genius. Herodotus was also a genius, but not of the same kind, and he did not have ten thousand men with him. He was an individual traveller and, in that country, he would have been an enemy alien lacking any pretext to account to the authorities for his journey except that of sheer curiosity. Moreover, this was not the way he travelled. He went where Greek traders went, and in their company. Greek traders found little to prevent them from visiting Greek cities round the coasts of the Black Sea or elsewhere, whether they were part of the Persian Empire or not, but to cross Armenia Herodotus would have had to travel with Persian, Median or Armenian traders, and he was totally unfitted for this kind of journey, besides having no gift for languages.

It is also virtually certain that he never travelled the royal road to Susa. He gives a detailed description of it, and of the stages along it, but he nowhere states that he travelled it himself. It was a much-travelled road, and he could easily have derived his information from a host of people who had had to make that journey on one mission or another. Moreover, it is hardly possible that Herodotus, if he had visited Susa, could have failed to say something of the city that would reveal that he had been there, but he nowhere does. All he does is to give a detailed description of an oil well in the village of Ardericca, about twenty-six miles from Susa, where Darius had settled some Eretrians whom his army had enslaved on its way to Marathon, but this is not enough. Besides, his description of the twisting course of the Euphrates in the vicinity of Ardericca—which is nowhere near that river—makes it clear that he was never in Ardericca either.

Since he never travelled the royal road, and since he never, either from there or from Myriandrus, crossed the multitudinous mountains to the coast of Pontus, and since he states unequivocally that he visited Colchis, it has to be concluded, though somewhat reluctantly, that he went there from Panticapaeum. He says nothing whatever of the places he passed or visited on his way there, but this is not unusual, since his book is a history, not a geography, and if his historical narrative, or some digressive topic he is pursuing, does not demand that a place should be mentioned he does not mention it, whether he was ever there or not. He says only that the journey to Phasis from the Sea of Azov would take a speedy traveller thirty days, the implication being that as a leisurely traveller he took longer. He exaggerates, since even in those days a determined traveller could certainly have done it in less.

From Panticapaeum to the city of Phasis, at the mouth of the river of the same name, was a voyage of about four hundred miles. Not far from the Strait of Kerch the land began to rise up steeply from the sea, and from then on he was sailing in the morning shadow of the Caucasus. The only city of any importance on this coast was the Milesian colony of Dioscurias, at the mouth of the river Anthemus. As they approached Phasis the mountains fell back to open up the plain of Colchis through which the river ran from its source in the mountains. Colchis is a triangular plain, hemmed in by mountains north and south, the coastline barely fifty miles long and the northern edge, below the Caucasus, less than a hundred. The river itself is a mere 180 miles long. In Herodotus's time its seaward end flowed through extensive marshes, but it was navigable for large vessels for about 38 miles from its mouth, and small vessels could go somewhat further. Its waters were noted for their purity. In modern times there is a hydroelectric plant near Kutaisi, sixty miles or so up-river, and the marshes of Colchis have largely been drained. The ancient city of Phasis is called Poti, and it is a major seaport of the West Georgian Soviet Socialist Republic, though it is no great rival to Batumi, forty miles to the south.

All this is a far cry from the Colchis of Greek legend. Here Jason came in the *Argo* with his heroic companions to bring back the golden fleece, which hung in an oak-tree in the grove of Ares and was guarded day and night by a dragon. Having reached Colchis after numerous adventures, Jason had to yoke two fire-breathing oxen with brazen feet to a plough, and overcome the warriors that sprang up when he sowed the teeth of the dragon slain by Cadmus in Thebes. Having done these things, and snatched the golden fleece from the oak-tree, Jason sailed away at night with the Colchian king's daughter, Medea, who chopped her little brother into pieces and threw them over the stern to delay pursuers. All this and more was told by Apollonius of Rhodes in his book on the voyage of the Argonauts, one of the most brilliant and readable books of antiquity, which Herodotus never had the pleasure of reading, since it was published two hundred years after his time. The legend was, however, familiar to him, and he speaks of the abduction of Medea from Colchis as one of the original causes of the quarrel between Persians and Greeks that led ultimately to the war between them.

Herodotus is more interested in events nearer his own age. At that time Colchis formed part of the Persian Empire, and paid tribute to Persia in the form of a hundred boys and a hundred girls every fourth year. Colchians had served in Xerxes' army, in which their soldiers wore wooden helmets, carried small rawhide shields and were armed with swords and short spears.

Herodotus's main aim there seems to have been to seek confirmation of his theory that the Colchians were descended from the Egyptian army that under Sesostris, as Herodotus believed, marched up this coast on their way to defeat the Scythians and Thracians. He is not sure whether the Egyptian ancestors of the Colchians were left behind by Sesostris because they were sick, or whether they deserted, but there could be no doubt, he says, that the Colchians were of Egyptian descent. One proof of it was that they had dark skins and woolly hair; another was that the Colchians themselves confirmed it— that is, they did not exactly confirm it, but they said they distinctly remembered the Egyptians. They remembered them, in fact, better than the Egyptians whom Herodotus interrogated in Egypt on the same subject remembered them, though the Egyptians, like himself, thought that the original Colchians were men of Sesostris's army. The third proof was that the Colchians, like the Egyptians and Ethiopians but no one else, had practised circumcision from ancient times.

It is difficult to make sense of anything Herodotus says about Colchis, or, for that matter, about Sesostris. It would be easy to dismiss the whole thing, saying that Herodotus never went there, and that when he says he asked some questions about this matter in Colchis he is simply lying, as he has been accused of doing on many other matters throughout the ages. On the other hand, he has been proved to have told the truth about so much that it would be a rash man who, retreating to Herodotus's bizarre theories about Colchis as to a last ditch, held that here, at least, he was telling lies. About the Colchians being dark-skinned and woolly-haired, at least, he may be right, since they were not—apart from the Greek settlers—an Indo-European people, and though not dark-skinned and woolly-haired to any great degree they may have been darker and woollier than anyone else that Herodotus had encountered up to that time.

As for the rest, it is possible that Herodotus was by then a little tired of taking in new impressions, as tends to happen towards the end of a long fact-finding journey; it is even more possible that the Colchians, on being addressed by this inquisitive young foreigner through an interpreter, agreed that their ancestors were Egyptians, whether they had heard of that people or not, simply to please him. Such a thing has happened to many other travellers in many other countries. It is unlikely that we shall ever get any nearer the truth of the Colchis episode.

From Colchis Herodotus returned to Panticapaeum and to Olbia, and from Olbia to the Bosphorus. It can safely be assumed that he did not sail home by the north coast of Asia Minor, past Pontus, Paphlagonia and Bithynia. This would be to entrust himself for too long a time to mariners of uncertain loyalties, and besides, that coast was notoriously dangerous to seafarers; so much so that the Greeks originally named the whole sea Pontos Axenos, the inhospitable sea, and only changed the name to Pontos Euxinos, the sea that is kindly to strangers, out of the same dislike for names of ill omen that made them change the name of the angry Fates, the Erinyes, to the Eumenides, the Gracious Ones.

For the next twenty-odd centuries all that was known about the Scythians was what Herodotus said about them, apart from the odd remark such as that attributed to Hippocrates, who is supposed to have said that they were inclined to laziness, fatness and gaiety; and Herodotus was regarded as an unreliable witness. Serious archaeological exploration of the burial mounds of south Russia and elsewhere began in the eighteenth century and has continued with growing intensity into the twentieth. During the same period further knowledge has been acquired of the Scythians and their southward incursions into Persia, Assyria and Babylonia from the decipherment of written records of that time. These investigations have endorsed in virtually every respect the account of Scythian life and history given by Herodotus at the same time as they have enlarged it.

Graves of the kings and chieftains, the people Herodotus called the royal Scythians who formed a ruling group dominating the neighbouring kindred nations, have been found over a very wide area of the steppe countries of western Asia and eastern Europe. They are numerous in the Kuban, north of the Caucasus, where they date from the seventh and sixth centuries B.C. The richest graves of a century later, the sixth and fifth centuries B.C., are those found in the Crimea and in south Russia, in the Taman peninsula and in the Dnieper valley as far up as Kiev, as well as in the Don, Donetz and Volga basins as far eastwards as the Urals. Others are found in the Danube basin as far west as Hungary and in what used to be East Prussia and is now western Poland. Much interest has been aroused in recent years by the excavations by the Russian archaeologists Gryazhnov, Rudenko and others in an area far to the east of the other royal Scythian tombs, at Pazyryk and other sites in the western Altai, nearer to Lake Baikal than to the Caspian. Here the ground is frozen throughout the winter but thaws in the brief summer. The mound of stones piled over the tomb prevented the underlying soil from being warmed up in summer, while water trickling down through the stones froze in winter, providing a permanent ice cover for the tomb's contents. Penetration of year-round sub-zero temperatures into the tomb itself was aided by the activities of grave-robbers who, digging from the top of the mound downwards, provided a channel for ice penetration into the burial chamber. Most of the tombs were rifled not long after the departure of the mourners, despite the surrounding guard of deceased and impaled horsemen, and most metal objects were taken, but textiles, leather and wooden objects remained in an extraordinary state of preservation. These Pazyryk tombs were of the sixth to the fourth centuries B.C., contemporary with those of Herodotus's royal Scythians of south Russia.

The Scythians were revealed by these investigations to modern eyes much as would be deduced from what Herodotus says of them, making allowance for his natural assumption that civilization was Greek civilization, and that the Scythians were interesting but on the whole rather dreary savages. They had an advanced nomad culture, and nomad cultures have lost out in the long run to settled crop-growing cultures, which make possible such things as cities, scholarship and sophisticated technologies. They were nevertheless highly skilled as horsemen, hunters, fishermen and farmers, when they chose to be farmers, and with a remarkable talent for the applied arts and crafts. They had no coinage and no written language, but carried on a far-flung trade with central Asia and with the Greek cities of Pontus, importing such things as ceramics, textiles, jewellery and other trinkets for wives, wine and oil in exchange for corn, hides, furs, timber and slaves. In their works of art animal motifs predominated, basically representational but formalized to produce harmonious designs and patterns. The favourite animal was a stag, the totem of many of the steppe nations, but other animals widely represented were horses, ibexes, boars, bears, wolves and tigers, besides eagles, fishes and mythological beasts such as lion-griffins and eagle-griffins. There were also some mythological scenes and geometrical patterns.

The tombs themselves were deep below ground level, the floor being typically about forty feet below the surface. The mounds covering them were from four hundred to twelve hundred feet in diameter. The walls of the tombs were faced with tree-trunks, matting, birch-bark, thatch or fabric In the Crimea the wall-covering material was often painted; in the Altai, wall-hangings were used There were hooks in the walls for spare clothing, and shelves for provisions The dead, wearing their finest clothes and jewellery, were arranged, as Herodotus described, on mattresses. These were laid east to west, sometimes on biers In the Altai tombs the bodies were often placed in coffins made of hollowed-out tree-trunks In some of the largest tombs several hundred horses were slaughtered to accompany the dead, being piled up in heaps around them Horses were mostly the small Mongolian ponies of the steppes, but in the Altai tombs some taller horses of Bactrian and Median breeds were found.

Drinking-skulls were found in many tombs, some of them mounted in intricately worked gold. Warriors wore bronze helmets and chain-mail jerkins of the Greek type, lined with red felt. Shields were usually round and made of leather, wood or iron, with a central boss often in the form of an animal, in gold. Bows, of the double-curved type, were carried in a bow-case slung from the left side of the belt, as was the quiver. Arrows, which were shot over the horse's left shoulder, or over its near quarter when the rider turned round in the saddle, had trefoil-shaped heads of bronze, iron or bone. Sword-blades were at first of bronze, later of iron, and the crosspieces were intricately ornamented. Sheaths found in tombs in south Russia were often covered with gold with embossed designs, inlaid with ivory and studded with gems. Daggers were attached to the left leg by straps. Many warriors carried spears, and others standards surmounted by figures of real or imaginary beasts in bronze.

Horse-trappings corresponded closely with Herodotus's descriptions. Some horses found at Pazyryk wore elaborate masks. Bridles had bronze or gold cheek-pieces in the shape of animals. Leather straps were ornamented with embossed, cut-out or appliqué designs, often featuring animals. Saddles consisted of two felt cushions mounted on wooden frames with yellow or red bindings, and sometimes embellished with gold plaques. Saddle-cloths were of felt ornamented with appliqué designs. Metal stirrups were not used, the rider's feet being supported by felt or leather loops.

Waggons were of the covered type with solid wheels and a central shaft to which the draught animals—usually oxen—were yoked in pairs.

Clothing was luxurious and liberally ornamented with embroidered or appliqué designs. The clothes of wealthy Scythians were sometimes covered with small gold sequins or embossed plaques, sewn on.

The wall-hangings of the Pazyryk tombs were ornamented with felt appliqué designs, some depicting the Great Goddess or other deities, some using animal motifs or geometrical patterns. In one tomb a Persian carpet of the fifth century B.C. was found, with a pattern depicting horsemen, elks and stars. Rugs were mostly of felt, as were mattresses and cushions. Other furniture included wooden tables with turned or carved legs and detachable tops, and wooden blocks serving as either stools or head-rests. There was a wide range of jewellery and gold ornaments.

Tattooing was apparently practised among the Scythians as among the Thracians, the embalmed body of a man found in one of the tombs being covered with tattooing, mostly lively representations of animals, mythical or real.

Every tomb contained at least one cast bronze cauldron of the distinctive Scythian shape, a hemispherical bowl resting on a truncated cone, around which the fire could be heaped. The upper rim had a number of handles shaped like animals, up to six, opposite each other in pairs. Some were quite small, others weighed up to 75 lbs. There were in addition the little cauldrons or incense-burners used for burning hemp-seeds.

Having recorded his observations of the Scythians in his notes, and in his mind, Herodotus sailed south, through the Bosphorus, the Marmara and the Hellespont, for the Aegean and Samos. His homeland of Halicarnassus, sixty miles further away down the coast, was still ruled by the tyrant Lygdamis, acting on the orders of the Persian governor at Sardis, and propped up by a Persian garrison. But the Greek world was stirring, ever more vigorously. Some time after Herodotus's return to Samos, and while he was still in his twenties, the movement to liberate his native city, in which he was deeply implicated, came to a head.

RETURN TO HALICARNASSUS

III

THE BATTLE OF PLATAEA in 479 B.C.—a year after Salamis—was by no means the end of the Persian war. It marked the turning-point where the Greeks, having against all possible odds defended their homeland against the great invasion under Xerxes, found it possible to do what, a year before, would hardly have been dreamed of: to go over to the offensive.

The Athenians, having returned to their city, which had been sacked and virtually destroyed by the Persians when the inhabitants fled to take refuge on the island of Salamis, began to rebuild the city and its walls, as well as those of its seaport Piraeus. The Spartans, dominant up to that time on the mainland, might have attempted to prevent by force the rebuilding of a walled city, as a possible rival so near the Peloponnese, if they had known of it; but Themistocles, in Sparta on an official visit, lulled Spartan suspicions with assurances that the walls would not be built, until they had reached such a stage in their building that it was too dangerous a task for the Spartans to attempt to pull them down.

The clearing of the Persian governors and garrisons from the trade routes to the Black Sea began. Sestos was besieged and fell in 478 B.C.; Pausanias liberated Byzantium, but his tyrannical behaviour led to his recall and the taking over of the naval leadership by the Athenians.

The destruction of Persian forces on land at Plataea and on sea at Mycale had made possible a gradual pushing back of Persian power from the eastern Mediterranean. To do this it was necessary to weld enough of the tiny city-states into an alliance capable of providing unified land and naval forces on a sufficient scale, and the main instrument by which this was achieved, under Athenian leadership, was the Delian League, whose formation began to take place from the years 478–77 B.C.

The Athenian leaders began to negotiate treaties of alliance with the city-states of the mainland and the islands. It was agreed that each state should make its contribution in money to the treasury of the Delian League which was located on Delos, probably in the great temple of Apollo to which the Hyperboreans of long ago had reputedly brought their offerings. Delos was also the seat of the council of the league. It was no doubt chosen because of its importance as a religious centre second only to Delphi, and preferable to Delphi on two grounds. The prophecies at Delphi and the policies of which they were an expression were, as has been said, persistently pro-Spartan; and Delos as a religious centre was particularly venerated by the Ionians both of the islands and of the Asian mainland, and therefore particularly suitable as the centre of a league among whose future aims must inevitably be the liberation of the Ionian cities.

The need for the league was clearly seen in these first years, and its growth was rapid. It numbered something like 150 member states by the end of 477 B.C. Athens was unequivocally the leader: the treaty with each state was bilateral between that state and Athens, and the states were forbidden to enter into treaties with each other. At first some states contributed ships as well as money, but it was Athens who decided which of them should do so. Athenian power was better served by contributions of money, which allowed her to increase the number of ships under her command, than by having in the fleet groups of ships owing prime loyalty to other states. After a few years it was only by permission of Athens that another state was allowed to maintain a fleet of its own at all.

The main purpose of the League was seen at first as a counter-attack against the Persians, and even with the expansion of its operations further afield the harrying of Persian possessions as an act of revenge, made more attractive by the possibilities of plunder, was a major impetus. Nevertheless an element of "imperialist" expansion was present at an early stage, as was seen when Cimon, commanding the naval forces, took the Persian fortress of Eion at the mouth of the River Strymon—that river which Xerxes' army had crossed up at Nine Ways, with the attendant sacrifice of eighteen teenage Thracians —and the island of Scyros, off Euboea. Athenian colonists were settled in both places, though Scyros was no part of the Persian Empire, its former inhabitants having been simple Pelasgian pirates whom the Athenian conquerors sold into slavery. Its capture had one sole motive, to increase the Athenian hold on the Aegean.

The abolition of piracy provided some justification for the annexation of Scyros, but harsher aspects of Athenian imperialism soon manifested themselves. The city of Carystus, on the south coast of Euboea, showed no inclination to join the League voluntarily, but since it occupied a strategic position poised on the Athenian sea-route across the Aegean, the Athenians captured it and compelled it to join. The island of Naxos went even further and seceded from the League, but was forcibly made to rejoin. The Athenian case was a strong one.

The Persian power was by no means destroyed; it was merely dormant under the continuing rule of the discouraged and demoralized Xerxes, who was content to pass the rest of his reign in superintending the building of Persepolis and occupying himself with his harem. But Xerxes would not reign for ever, and a unified Greek power was a necessity. It has been the tragedy throughout Greek history that the need for such unity has warred constantly against the precious Greek gift of individualism, and the difficult art of reconciling the two has never been mastered.

During the first ten years of the Delian League, while it was growing in strength under the sometimes less than universally acceptable rule of Athens, Persian power was recovering too. News of a gathering of their forces was brought to Athens, and Cimon sailed with his fleet to Pamphylia, the bend of what is now the Turkish coast east of Antalya, to forestall their preparations. There, near the mouth of what was then the Eurymedon and is now the Köprü Su or Bridgewater, running from between the big lakes of Eğridir and Beyşehir south to the sea past the spectacular ruins of Aspendos, he decisively defeated the Persians by both land and sea. This crushing victory in 469 B.C. is often regarded as the final engagement of the Greco-Persian war, but the struggle continued in various guises till 449 B.C., not without some setbacks for the Athenians. It can be said, however, that it marks the beginning of the final phase, during most of which Athens had the upper hand.

The victory brought little joy to the Spartans. They saw it as a further enlargement of the already dangerous sea power of Athens, which by now more than counterbalanced their own strength by land. The deepening enmity of Sparta and Athens had other causes besides that of the tilting of the balance of power in favour of Athens. Sparta was a rigid oligarchy, and the increasing advance of democratic ideas of government in Athens was feared as a potential danger to the stability of the Spartan state.

A few years after the victory at the Eurymedon, in 465, Xerxes was assassinated by the commander of his bodyguard, and succeeded by his brother as Artaxerxes I. Artaxerxes had his hands full for some time with the business of putting down the numerous revolts that inevitably arose here and there in his realms.

In 465 another dependency of the Athenian Empire grew restless and seceded from the League. This time it was Thasos, an island noted for its gold mines, lying off the Thracian coast east of the Strymon. The Athenians laid siege to the city of Thasos; the Thasians asked the Spartans to help them by invading Attica. The Spartans secretly promised to aid them, but were prevented from doing so by two disastrous events, a major earthquake in Laconia itself, the heartland of Sparta, and a revolt of the helots in Laconia and Messenia, further west. The revolt in Laconia was savagely put down, but that in Messenia rumbled on for some years.

In 463 B.C. a large Athenian colony settled further up the Strymon river from Eion at its mouth, at that same locality of Enneahodoi or Nine Ways, the future site of Amphipolis, where Xerxes and his army had crossed the river. Other colonists penetrated still further up-river to a place called Drabescus. The local Thracian tribe, the Edonians, noted for their wild Bacchic orgies, saw themselves being gradually dispossessed and driven out as the Greeks moved inland, and this latest incursion was more than they could tolerate. They launched such a devastating attack on the new colony that not only were most of the settlers wiped out but those at Nine Ways lost confidence in the colony's future and had to be withdrawn. The event caused some loss of faith in Cimon's leadership, despite his naval victory over the Thasians and his conquest of their city, which after two years' siege had to surrender. Public figures, particularly Greek public figures, cannot afford one failure, however distinguished their previous run of successes. However, Cimon was still in command, and inflicted harsh peace terms on the defeated Thasians, who had to surrender the whole of their fleet, destroy all the fortifications of their city and pay a large annual tribute.

The Spartans and the Athenians were still officially allies, the treaty of alliance against the Persians entered into in 481 B.C. being still unrevoked. The Spartans now issued a general appeal to all their allies to come and aid them in putting down the helot revolt. Cimon, a genial and large-minded character, believed that peaceful co-existence between Athens and Sparta, the sea-power and the land-power, was not only possible but necessary. Pursuing this policy, he led an army to the aid of the Spartans. The Spartans, welcoming aid from their other allies, were deeply suspicious of Athenian motives, and politely declined to make use of Cimon and his army. This refusal of the aid offered was considered an insult in Athens, and an immediate effect was a further sharp drop in Cimon's popularity. A new star was rising in Athens, the young Pericles, whose anti-Spartan policy at this time was more to the taste of the Athenians than Cimon's attempts to preserve what had formerly been a friendship, though often an uneasy one.

Cimon had displaced Themistocles in the hard world of Athenian politics, and Themistocles had sought refuge in Persia. There Arta-xerxes had made him governor of Magnesia, where he lived on in exile until he died in 449 B.C. at the age of sixty-five. Now it was

Herodotus's Eastern Pilgrimage through Assyro-Babylonia

Ancient drinking horn with a
crouched griffin base.

The River Euphrates passing a village near Babylon which Herodotus visited on his long pilgrimage through Assyro-Babylonia.

Cimon's turn. He was tried and ostracized, that is, sent into banishment by the people's vote, inscribed on potsherds: *ostrakon* being a potsherd or tile.

The Spartans finally got the better of the Messenian helots, but these surrendered only on terms that allowed them to leave the Peloponnese. The Athenians welcomed them as allies and settled them at Naupactus in Locris. Meanwhile the Athenians had also acquired as allies Argos and Thessaly, the principal enemies of Sparta. Megara too deserted the Peloponnesian League to enter into alliance with Athens.

Athenian expansionism was in full swing in these years of Pericles' rise to power from 461 B.C., when he was instrumental in the measures that weakened the influence of the Areopagus, the conservative body of elders that was seen as standing in the way of democratic progress.

At this time Inarus, a Libyan king, revolted against the Persian rulers to whom he was subject, and asked the Athenians for aid. In 460 a great Athenian expedition sailed for Egypt; other Athenian expeditionary forces were fighting at the same time in Cyprus and in Phoenicia, not to mention wars nearer home in Megara and in Aegina. The Athenians landed a force in the Peloponnese itself, in Argolis, but were thrown back there by the men of Corinth and Epidaurus; but they were victorious in a naval battle off Aegina, and defeated the Corinthians in Megara. There was, in fact, by 459 B.C. a full-scale war between Athens and her allies on the one hand and Sparta and her allies on the other. This period from 459 to 446 is often referred to as the First Peloponnesian War, a precursor of the greater struggle that began after an uneasy fifteen-year interval.

In all this wild explosion of activity, when all the Greeks in the world seemed to be surging up, fighting their enemies abroad and fighting each other at home, what was happening across the Aegean in Ionia passed almost without notice. However, stirring events were taking place there too. Some time in these years—the date cannot be accurately determined—Herodotus, the young traveller back in Samos from his journey to the remote north, joined the forces that were being got together there for the liberation of Halicarnassus. And some time in those years he sailed from Samos to take part in that liberation and in the overthrow of the tyrant Lygdamus.

Halicarnassus, a free city-state once more, joined the Delian League. In mainland Greece, the war between Athens and Sparta increased in scale and ferocity. The men of Phocis, allies of Athens from north of the Gulf of Corinth, attacked the Doric people in Doris, to the west of them. A Spartan army crossed the Gulf to go to the help of their kinsmen and forced the Phocians to withdraw. The Spartans marched into Boeotia and renewed their alliance with Thebes. The Athenians marched north to attack them at Thebes, and the two armies met in a fierce battle at Tanagra. The Athenians got rather the worse of it, but they gained more in the long run, since the Spartans marched home, pillaging Megara on the way, while the Athenians raised another army and defeated the Boeotians, whom the Spartans had left unsupported behind them. The Boeotians, the Phocians and others renewed their alliance with Athens, and the result of the Spartan incursion was finally the consolidation of Athenian power in central Greece.

This was in 457 B.C. Three years later the Egyptian expedition ended in disaster with the re-establishment of Persian rule there. Much of the advantage over the Persians that had been gained by the victory at the Eurymedon seemed to be lost again; the Athenian fleet had suffered great losses in ships and men, and the Phoenician fleet was able to venture once again west of Cyprus, for the first time since 469 B.C. The treasury of the Delian League was transferred for greater security from Delos to Athens; it had been the last remnant of any importance of Delos in the league named after it, since the council of the League had long since ceased to meet. There was no longer even a pretence that the decisions of the League lay with any power but Athens.

Cimon was recalled from his exile to command a fleet sailing to Cyprus. Cimon died during the campaign, while besieging Citium, but it ended in a Greek victory north of the modern Famagusta that redressed the failure of the Egyptian expedition and, even more important, made possible the conclusion of a peace treaty with Persia. This was negotiated by one Callias, who had fought at Marathon forty years before, in 490. The treaty was concluded in 449 on terms somewhat less favourable to the Persians than might have been expected, though the Athenians had to acknowledge Persian possession of Cyprus and of Egypt. Despite his diplomatic triumph, Callias, on returning to Athens, was accused of taking bribes and fined fifty talents.

Herodotus had willingly played his part in the liberation of his native city, but this is not to say that he found perfect satisfaction in living there. A returning exile sees much about his native country that the person who has never left it does not see, but this does not mean that he is welcomed as bringing a superior wisdom to the conduct of affairs. It does not even mean that he is better qualified to conduct them. A Halicarnassian may see things in a certain light, and wish to be governed by men who see them in a similar light, not by men who have acquired a different point of view in Samos. Not that it was necessarily his period of exile that militated against his success in Halicarnassian politics; in any politics, and all the more in Greek politics, to be the man who comes out on top requires certain qualities exercised in a certain way at a certain time, and he who has them is not necessarily the wisest. If he were, the whole course of human history would have been different.

Herodotus, though a member of a leading family of Halicarnassus, may not have had any great wish to shoulder the responsibilities of state. He had other interests, and the journey to Scythia had by no means quenched his thirst for travel. Some time between 454 and 449 B.C., when he was aged between thirty and thirty-five, he set off again, this time for the east.

Both the order and the dates of his second and third major journeys —to Babylon and to Egypt—are indeterminable from direct evidence, and have to be deduced from the chronology of known events and from occasional statements made by Herodotus himself in his own chronicle. As to the order, it seems certain that he must have gone to Babylon first. The principal evidence for this is a remark he makes (ii, 156) when describing the lake of Moeris in Egypt. He says he asked the people who lived there what was done with the earth dug out when the lake was excavated, since he could see no sign of it. They told him it was thrown into the Nile, which carried it away. This, he says, reminded him of a similar story he heard in Babylon: how some thieves who stole a treasure from Sardanapalus's underground strong-room did so by digging a tunnel to it, and concealed what they were doing by throwing the earth they dug out into the Tigris at night, so that no one would begin to wonder where it came from.

It has been suggested that, having been first to Egypt, and later to Babylonia, he visited Egypt a second time, and it was on this second occasion that his reminiscence of Babylon was prompted. The idea is that he went from Egypt to Tyre to make certain enquiries from the priests of the temple of Heracles there. While in Tyre he took the opportunity of going off down the Euphrates to Babylon, and after-wards returned to Egypt. It is ingenious, like the phlogiston theory— if something weighs more after phlogiston has left it, phlogiston must have a negative weight—but, like the phlogiston theory, it arouses instant scepticism. The journey to Babylon was a remarkable one, perhaps more taxing than the journey to Scythia, since in Scythia he was at least in neutral territory, where Greeks, if not exactly welcomed, were accepted, and widespread; whereas the journey to Babylon took him deep into what was, at least in theory, a country held by the enemy. The idea that, finding himself in Tyre, he casually slipped down to Babylon and back, before returning to Egypt, is not in accordance with the state of things at the time. From Egypt to Tyre was a simple enough journey; to visit Tyre on his way home from Egypt, or even to go to Tyre and return to Egypt again, was no great matter. But to travel on to Babylon was a matter requiring a great deal of arranging, and Tyre was no place to arrange it. Even if Herodotus had felt the inclination to cross great tracts of the Syrian desert in order to get to the Euphrates, he would have found no one in Tyre who shared it. He would have had to move a few hundred miles up the coast before he could find anyone who was even interested in talking about going to Babylon, and by then he would certainly have lost any lingering notions about going back to Egypt. To travel from Egypt to Babylon via Tyre would be like going to the moon, not even directly from earth, but after a whimsical digression to some other heavenly body on the way.

His conversation by Lake Moeris may, therefore, be taken as good circumstantial evidence that he went to Babylon first, without a prior visit to Egypt. The difficulty then is, of course—and hence the theory of a dual visit to Egypt—the time factor. Herodotus cannot very well have visited Egypt during the insurrection there against the Persians that lasted from 460 to 454 B.C., even if he had not made it clear in his own narrative that he went there after the insurrection was over. He went there after 454; but the Peace of Callias with Persia was not concluded until 449, and it is reasonably certain that by 446 he was in Athens.

He could quite easily have fitted in his journey to Egypt between 449 and 446, but could he have visited Babylon too? He would have had to leave Halicarnassus the moment the Peace of Callias was signed in 449; dash down to Babylon and back; hasten off to Egypt, either with or without a hurried excursion to Halicarnassus to greet his family; then bustle back again, calling in at Tyre on the way, and, after a final word with his family, rush off to Athens to be there in time for the public reading of his works scheduled for 446.

We are in the wrong century for an itinerary of this kind. It is clear that Herodotus must have left Halicarnassus for his journey to Babylon —since this preceded the Egyptian one—some years before the signing of the Peace of Callias in 449, in order to fit in all this travelling in the leisurely way to which—with his habit of chatting to all and sundry along the way—he was obviously accustomed.

The remaining difficulty is that before 449 B.C. the Greeks and the Persians were still at war, but its solution lies in the nature of that war. There was no such thing as total war at that time, or for something getting on for two and a half thousand years to come. Apart from actual battle zones, people could, and did, move about from one empire to another. Themistocles, whose advice had been largely responsible for the victory at Salamis, fled, after his fall from power and his ostracism in 471, from Argos to Corcyra, thence to Epirus and finally to Ephesus, in the dominions of the Great King. He travelled across those dominions to visit Artaxerxes himself in Susa. This was in 465, when the war had still sixteen years to run.

Herodotus might have been ill-advised to visit Egypt between 460 and 454, when the Athenians were actively intervening on the side of a rebellion against Persian rule, and he had been obliged to flee from Samos in his late teens because he was suspected of plotting against the local tyrant, but there was little to prevent him from landing in a quiet Phoenician city on the shores of the Mediterranean, where war and the rumours of war were far away, merely because Phoenicia happened to be ruled for the time being by the Persians, just as it had previously been ruled by the Assyrians and the Babylonians and would subsequently be ruled by the Macedonians and the Romans. That city contained a large community of Greeks who, as long as they were engaged in peaceful pursuits, could come and go on their own business, as they had done in the past and would go on doing in the future. He needed no passport, neither did he need a Babylonian phrase-book. He landed from a Greek ship in a city where many Greeks lived, where there were men who would tell the guards on the quay who he was, and vouch for him, if they were asked to; and everywhere he travelled he would find someone who spoke some sort of Greek, to tell him what he wanted to know.

If, from that Phoenician city, he took a fancy to travel inland to the Euphrates, and down the Euphrates to Babylon, there was an element of risk, certainly, but probably less risk than there had been from the storms of the Black Sea. He would certainly find, in such a town, Greeks who now and then made that journey, with no more desperate end in view than commerce; and they would, no doubt for a consideration, take him along with them.

So it was that, having a whim to visit Babylon, Herodotus, being then between thirty and thirty-five years of age, sailed from Halicarnassus, bound for Myriandrus on the Gulf of Issus.

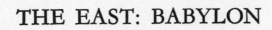

IV

HERODOTUS WENT TO Myriandrus because, for a Greek who wanted to visit Babylon, and had no particular mission to account for a journey along the Royal Road from Sardis to Susa, through the heart of the Persian Empire in wartime, that was the only convenient and practical way of getting there.

It was a Phoenician city. The Phoenicians, like the Greeks, were great sailors. The Greeks, in fact, had learned about sailing from them, just as they had also learned the Semitic alphabet from them and adapted it to their own language. They had planted colonies all over the Mediterranean, as the Greeks did later, the greatest being at Carthage in North Africa; but their colonies were to be found beyond the Pillars of Hercules, on the west coasts of Spain and of North Africa. Their traders had visited the Scilly Islands and Cornwall and established with the rude Britons a flourishing trade in tin.

In more recent times they had supplied most of the naval forces of the Persian Empire, the rest being mostly made up of Ionians. They lived in a country never more than a few miles broad and little more than a hundred miles long, stretching from the northern border of the modern Lebanon as far south as the modern Haifa; roughly speaking, their homeland was the coast of Lebanon. Aradus, Byblus, Berytus (Beirut), Sidon, Tyre and Acre were its chief cities. They spoke a dialect of Aramic and wrote in the Samaritan or ancient Hebrew letters. They were a cultivated people long before the Indo-European horsemen invaded Greece from the north and became Greeks; Hiram, the Phoenician king of Tyre, sent architects and artists to assist Solomon in building the temple at Jerusalem.

Myriandrus was a Phoenician colony on the coast of Syria, on the Gulf of Issus, a few miles south of the site of the modern Iskenderun. From there to the Euphrates was a journey of a hundred miles eastwards across northern Syria: in contrast to the journey from Tyre, which would have been a journey of five hundred miles across a country not quite as desert as it is now, but desolate enough. Certainly caravans laden with goods from the east crossed it, and just as certainly Herodotus did not.

The Euphrates rises in the Palandöken mountains south of Erzurum and flows into the Tigris about sixty miles from the Persian Gulf, having passed through the site of ancient Babylon on the way. Herodotus, having travelled overland from Myriandrus, reached it somewhere around the present Turkish frontier, no great distance from Carchemish, and about six hundred miles upstream from Babylon.

The first thing he noticed about the great river was something which surprised him, he says, more than anything except the city of Babylon itself. This was the peculiar cargo-boats used to transport goods from the upper reaches of the river, in distant Armenia, down to Babylon. They were circular in shape, being made of hides stretched over a framework of withies. These vessels, resembling ancient British (and, in quite recent times, Welsh) coracles in shape and construction, were assembled in Armenia. Having been filled with straw and loaded with the cargo, which was principally wine in palm-wood casks, they were allowed to float downstream with the current, aided by the efforts of the two-man crew, each one wielding a paddle. The ront man drew the paddle through the water towards him, the rear man pushed the water away from him with his, and both presumably used the paddle to prevent the coracle from spinning round and round. The coracles varied greatly in size, the biggest having a capacity of about fourteen tons. Besides the crew of two men, each boat carried at least one donkey, the largest carrying several.

On reaching Babylon the cargo was sold and the boat was broken up, since it was impossible to paddle back upstream against the current. The frames and straw were sold and the donkeys were used to transport the hides back overland to Armenia. In Armenia, fresh boats were built to the same pattern, using the same hides.

Travelling down to Babylon—not in one of the circular cargo-boats, though in what kind of boat he travelled he does not say—Herodotus observed the country around him with his usual acuity. It was, he said, the richest grain-bearing country in the world; no figs, grapes or olives were grown there, and no fruit trees of any kind, but the fields were so fertile that the crop yields were two hundred times the weight of the seed sown in an average year, and in an exceptional year could be as much as three hundred times. The leaves of the wheat and barley were three inches across. He refused to record in his book the size to which millet and sesame grew, having found that people who had not been to Babylonia refused to believe him. The result of this astonishing fertility was that Babylonia produced a third of the supplies for the whole of the Persian Empire. The personal establishment of the governor of Babylonia, he found later, reflected this wealth; he received forty bushels of silver a day—

320 gallons, dry measure—and with it maintained, among other details of his retinue, eight hundred stallions and sixteen thousand mares.

This great abundance of grain was produced despite the inadequate rainfall, which, Herodotus says, was enough to germinate the seed but not enough to swell the grain. The balance of the necessary moisture was made up by irrigation. The whole country was criss-crossed with dykes, from which the water was lifted and poured into irrigation channels in the fields by means of the device still to be seen in Egypt and elsewhere in the Near East, the shaduf. This consists of a bucket or dipper fastened to a fifteen-foot-long counterpoised beam which in its turn is supported on a three-foot-high pivot, so that the bucket can be dipped in the canal or dyke, raised, swung and emptied into the irrigation channel

The elaborate and complex irrigation network of Herodotus's time was extensively damaged in the strife of succeeding centuries, particularly after the Arab incursions from the time of the rise of Islam. His description of Mesopotamia's remarkable fertility is amply confirmed by documentation in Parthian and Roman times, and by archaeological evidence. Irrigation schemes in modern times have not yet succeeded in restoring more than a small fraction of the former productivity of this region.

The sesame crop was used to produce oil, the only oil used in the country. Date-palms, which grew everywhere, produced "food, wine and honey"; Herodotus apparently does not reckon them to come in the category of fruit-trees. They were cultivated in the same way as the Greeks cultivated figs, by binding the flower of the male tree into that of the female or date-bearing tree. Herodotus has an ingenious explanation of his own for this simple method of fertilization, familiar to growers of marrows: his theory was that the gall-fly present in the male fruit was able to enter the female fruit and, by ripening it, prevent it from dropping off. Literally speaking this is more or less correct, but the suspicion remains that the role of the gall-fly was not wholly understood.

He describes the dress of the Babylonians, though the people he has in mind are clearly those of the more wealthy and leisured classes in the cities, and more particularly in Babylon itself. They wore, he says, a long linen tunic reaching down to the feet, with a woollen tunic over it and, over that, a short white cloak. Their shoes resembled Boeotian slippers, and they wore turbans; they grew their hair long and perfumed themselves all over. Every man had his own seal, and everyone carried a walking-stick specially made for him, with a device carved on the top, such as an apple, a rose, a lily or an eagle.

With his description of marriage customs he is back in the villages
that he passed on his way down river. In every village the girls who
had reached marriageable age were gathered together once a year, and
all the men stood round in a circle. An auctioneer, calling on each one
in turn to stand up, offered her for sale to the highest bidder. He
started always with the most attractive girl and went on to the second
best as soon as he had got a good price for the first. Wealthy men bid
eagerly against each other for the prettiest girls; by the time it came
down to the less appealing ones the humbler peasants, who needed a
hard-working wife rather than a good-looking one, were actually
paid to take them away. The auctioneer came last of all to the plainest
girls and the deformed or crippled. These would be knocked down
one by one to whoever would accept the smallest payment for taking
them. The money for these payments came from the sale of the more
attractive girls, whose attractions in this way were made to provide
dowries for the less fortunate.

The law forbade a man to marry his daughter off to someone of his
own choice; she had to take her part in the auction. A man who had
acquired a girl in this way was not allowed to take her home with him
until he had produced a guarantor to confirm his intention of marrying her.

Herodotus thought this an admirable custom, and it has a certain
measure of justice in it, though it has its rough aspects. He says,
however, that by the time of his visit it had largely fallen into disuse,
and girls of the poorer classes usually took up prostitution for a living.
This change had resulted from the Persian conquest with all the social
disruption and poverty which it brought to the countryside in its
train.

One custom Herodotus regarded as utterly shameful. Every woman
who was a native of the country was required once in her life to go
and sit in the temple of Aphrodite until a man came and selected her
by throwing a silver coin into her lap, saying "In the name of the
goddess Mylitta", this being the name of the original Assyrian
goddess whom the Greeks regarded as the equivalent of their own
Aphrodite. The woman had no choice in the matter, but had to go
outside with the first man who threw this money into her lap, and lie
with him. Once she had done so her duty to the goddess was dis-
charged and she was allowed to return home. From then on no offer,
however large, was sufficient to seduce her. Attractive women soon
performed this ceremony and got home again, but unattractive ones
might have to stay in the temple a long time before they were chosen,
stays of three or four years being not unknown.

Another custom in marriage was that when a man had had intercourse with his wife he had to sit and fumigate himself over an incense burner, and his wife had to do the same. Until they had done this they were not allowed to touch any household utensils.

There were, according to Herodotus, no doctors in Babylonia. When a man was ill he was taken out into the street, and anyone who passed by advised how he should be treated, either from his own experience or from his knowledge of how a similar condition had been successfully treated in someone else. No one was allowed to pass by in silence; everyone was required to ask what was the matter with the sick person, and suggest remedies.

The dead were buried in honey, and dirges were sung over them similar to those Herodotus later heard in Egypt.

Apart from these customs in marriage, sickness and burial Herodotus mentions one diet that struck him as being of peculiar interest. There were three tribes of the Babylonian people who lived entirely on fish: these were dried in the sun, after which the flesh was pounded in a mortar, sifted through muslin, and either kneaded into cakes or baked.

The first place Herodotus passed on his way down the Euphrates was Carchemish. It was hereabouts that the Babylonians, having destroyed Nineveh with the aid of their allies the Medes in 612 B.C., defeated an Egyptian army under the king Necho in 605, and so established themselves as rulers in this part of the world, and heirs of the Assyrians. Their empire did not last long, since Cyrus the Persian conquered them sixty-six years later, in 539. Carchemish was a site much investigated by early twentieth-century archaeologists, and among those who assisted them was the young T. E. Lawrence, a year or two before World War I.

Further downstream the river made its great bend to the east, and along this east–west stretch they passed Thapsacus, or Thiphsach, a name derived from the Aramaic word for a ford, this being in fact the last place at which the river could be forded.

Two hundred and fifty miles downstream from Carchemish the tributary called Chaboras flowed into the Euphrates from the north. The river was called by Xenophon the Araxes—one of several rivers which have been given that name by one writer or another, though this is a very dubious claimant—and at its confluence with the Euphrates stood in later years the town of Circesium, which was the ultimate border town of the Roman Empire; though there was an outpost fifty miles lower down at Durah, a town founded by the Macedonians. That fortress, having been in Roman hands since A.D. 165, was stormed and destroyed by the Sassanians under Shahpur I in 256. There have been more empires, probably, in this land of the two rivers than in any other corner of the earth.

A hundred miles further down, on the left bank of the Euphrates, was the town of Is, on the river of the same name; it is now called Hit. In this neighbourhood, about eight days' journey by boat from Babylon, were the "springs of asphalt" from which the bitumen was obtained that was used instead of mortar in building the walls of Babylon. Herodotus remarks that lumps of bitumen were found in great quantities in the river here.

Sixty miles lower down they passed the place where the Median Wall came down to the river. This was a mighty wall running from the Euphrates to the Tigris, which here began to approach each other more closely. It was often regarded as the dividing line between Babylonia and Mesopotamia; though dividing lines here mean even less than in most places, and in an earlier age it was the heart of the ancient realm of Akka. Xenophon describes the Median Wall as being about seventy miles long, a hundred feet high and twenty feet thick, and built of baked bricks joined together with asphalt. He certainly exaggerates the length, which was about fifty miles, and probably the other dimensions. It was, nevertheless, an impressive monument, and like many of the other works of man, over a wide area reaching as far up as Armenia, whose origin was lost to memory, it was regarded as having been built by Semiramis.

So many marvels were attributed to this lady that learned and sceptical men concluded that she was entirely legendary. She built the great works by which water was brought down to the citadel at Van; she built the city of Babylon and all its marvels, including the Hanging Gardens; she built other walls, cities and waterworks all over the Near East, conquered Egypt, Ethiopia and most of the nations of Asia, and at last, turning herself into a dove, flew up to heaven.

It is true that she did none of these things. Nor did she found Nineveh with a husband Ninus, whom she never married since he never existed. She was not even the daughter of the fish-goddess Derceto. Nevertheless, she existed, or at least a real woman on whom all these legends were pinned existed, and she must presumably have had an outstanding personality to attract so many stories. She was called Samuramat, and was what is usually politely called the queen of Samsi-Adad V, king of Assyria, though one of the first pieces of evidence of her real existence, an inscription on a column deciphered about 1909, describes her simply as "A woman of the palace of Samsi-Adad, King of the World, King of Assyria". After Samsi-Adad died, she acted as regent from 809 to 806 B.C., during the minority of her son; so, if not a queen, she was at least mother of a king.

Herodotus had no doubt at all of her existence. He does not say much about her, merely remarking that many of the kings who ruled

Babylon improved its defences and adorned its temples, and so also did two queens, of whom the earlier—Semiramis—preceded the later —Nitocris—by about five generations. He mentions some flood-control measures undertaken by her, and goes on to remark that the later queen, Nitocris, was a woman of greater intelligence than Semiramis. His estimate of the gap in generations between them is not far from the mark, though perhaps seven would have been nearer. However, the fact that Herodotus thought Semiramis existed was not regarded by historians as evidence that she did, rather the contrary, and until the inscriptions came along they were much happier to regard her as a fish-goddess.

Forty miles or so below the Median Wall was the entrance to the canal that joined the Euphrates to the Tigris here, where they were hardly more than twenty miles apart. This was the largest of the irrigation works mentioned by Herodotus, and he rightly remarks of it that it was so broad it could only be crossed by boat; it was called the Royal Canal, and it was navigable over the whole of its length.

Periodic flooding of the plain through which the Tigris and Euphrates run in the lower part of their courses has always been a problem, and one of the earliest persons to devote herself to attempts to overcome this menace was Semiramis. She built certain embankments in the plain outside the city to control the floodwaters. The later queen, Nitocris, not content with her predecessor's embankments, cut a winding channel for the river instead of its previous straight one, to reduce the speed of the current, and had exceptionally broad and high embankments constructed along both banks. She also had a large basin dug out a long way above the city, using the earth dug out to raise the height of the embankments. The basin was faced with stone, and water was apparently diverted into it from the main stream in times of danger from flooding.

Having sailed past the great works of Semiramis and Nitocris, Herodotus came to the city of Babylon. It had been destroyed by the Assyrians under Sennacherib—Ionians served in his army—in 689 B.C., but was rebuilt and reached the pinnacle of its splendour under Nebuchadnezzar—strictly speaking Nebuchadrezzar, but the "n" is hallowed not only by usage but by prosody; the persons who preferred it showed excellent taste—son of Nabopolassar, the victor over the Egyptians at Carchemish.

Herodotus describes it as lying in a wide plain, an immense city in the form of a square with sides nearly fourteen miles long, its circumference being about fifty-six miles. Besides being of enormous size, it surpassed in splendour any city in the known world. It was surrounded by a wall which Herodotus describes as thirty feet thick and a hundred and twenty feet high, and outside the wall was a deep and broad moat. When the moat was being dug, according to Herodotus, the earth shovelled out was baked into bricks some of which—using the bitumen from Is as a mortar—were used to revet the walls of the moat. The rest were used in the construction of the walls. Rush mats were laid between each thirty courses of bricks, both in revetting the moat and in building the wall. On the top of the wall a line of one-roomed buildings, facing inwards, was constructed along each edge. There was enough room for a four-horse chariot to pass between them. There were a hundred gates in the wall, all of bronze with bronze uprights and lintels.

The Euphrates ran through the middle of the city, dividing it into two. The outer wall of the city came down to the water's edge on both sides, and another wall of baked bricks without mortar ran along the river's bank through the town. Many of the houses in the city had three or four stories. The main streets, and the cross-streets leading to the river, were all perfectly straight and at right angles to each other, and at the end of each cross-street there was a bronze gate in the river wall to give access to the river.

The main wall was the chief defence of the city, but within it was a second one, hardly less strong. In the middle of each half of the city was a major building, in one half the royal palace, surrounded by a strong wall of its own, and in the other the temple of Bel, whom Herodotus describes as the Babylonian equivalent of Zeus. The temple, which Herodotus says was still in existence at the time of his visit, was a square building, each of its sides a quarter of a mile in length, with bronze gates. It had a solid central tower an eighth of a mile square surmounted by a second tower slightly smaller, which in its turn was surmounted by a third and so on up to eight towers in all. The towers could be climbed by a spiral staircase running round the outside. There were seats half-way up for people climbing the towers to rest on. On the summit stood a great temple containing no image, only a large couch, richly covered, with a golden table standing beside it. Herodotus was told that a different Assyrian woman was chosen by the god every day to spend the night there alone. During the night the god entered the temple in person and spent the night on the couch, presumably with the woman. Herodotus says there were instances of a similar custom in the Egyptian temple to the equivalent of Zeus at the Egyptian Thebes, and also at Patara in Lycia. The temple is now the largest mound on the site of Babylon, and is known to the Arabs as Babil.

At a lower level in the temple at Babylon there was a second shrine with a large seated figure of Bel, of gold, on a golden throne, on a

A girl farm-hand from Saqqâra near Memphis is carrying home harvest fruits and vegetables in her crescent-shaped Nile papyrus reed basket and holding a young gazelle in her arms. Herodotus, the engaging conversationalist, was ever eager to spend time talking to women from all walks of life as he found them to be excellent respondents. This Memphis maid would have provided him with data concerning domestic and agricultural Egyptian country life as well as the religious and social mores of Egyptian women.

golden plinth, with a golden table beside it. Herodotus was told that these objects contained more than twenty-two tons of gold. Outside the temple there were two more altars, one of gold on which sucklings were sacrificed, and one—larger but not of gold—on which fully grown sheep were sacrificed. On the larger one some two and a half tons of frankincense were consumed during the festival of Bel. In the time of Cyrus the temple also contained a solid gold statue of a man fifteen feet high, but it was no longer there. Darius had thought of carrying it off, but his courage failed him; after him, Xerxes not only took away the statue but killed the priest who tried to prevent him from doing so.

Nitocris, the lady who was more sensible than Semiramis, was also responsible for bridging the Euphrates in the city itself so that the inhabitants could get from one half to the other without the inconvenience of climbing into boats and rowing across. She had immense blocks of stone prepared beforehand, while the lake designed for flood control was being excavated. When it was dug out, she had the river diverted into it. While it was filling up and the river bed within the city was dry, she had an embankment of baked bricks built on each side of the river where it flowed through the city, and also paved with bricks the sloping roads leading down to the river from the gates at the end of the cross-streets. Then she had the piers built for a bridge across the river as near as possible to the centre of the town, using the blocks she had had prepared, bound together with iron and lead. Square wooden platforms were laid on the piers to form a bridge during the day, but at night they were removed to prevent people from crossing from one side to the other to commit robberies. When the embankments and the bridge were finished the Euphrates was restored to its normal course.

Nitocris was one of those royal persons otherwise almost unknown in antiquity and extremely rare in more recent centuries who have been gifted with a sense of humour, a quality usually blotted out by the high degree of self-esteem encouraged by the profession. Hers was of the more macabre variety. She had a tomb made for herself above one of the main gateways into the city, and had carved on it the following inscription: "If any ruler of Babylon after me is short of money, let him open my tomb and take as much as he wants. But he must only do this if he is really in need, otherwise it will do him no good."

Nobody disturbed her rest until Darius, when he put down the Babylonian revolt, came to the city. He did not like the idea of driving in and out under Nitocris's dead body, and this meant he was unable to use this gate; but it infuriated him even more to think that there was a treasure lying idle up there when he could quite easily take it

D

for himself. So he had the tomb opened, but found no treasure of any kind inside, only the body of Nitocris and another inscription, which read: "If you had not been insatiably greedy for money, and willing to use any means whatever to get it, you would not have broken open the tomb of the dead."

Nabopolassar, the first king of the Chaldean dynasty of Babylonia, reigned from 625 to 605 B.C. His eldest son was Nebuchadnezzar, a name signifying: "O Nabu, Protect my Boundary Stone". He was the second of the name. When young, he worked as a labourer in the restoration of the temple of Marduk. It is said that he married a Median princess and built the Hanging Gardens to satisfy her yearning for her native hills. They were an artificial hill of terraced gardens built up over a vaulted sub-structure, and were renowned in Hellenistic times as one of the seven wonders of the world. They were probably situated in the northerly part of the city, near the Ishtar Gate, east of the Euphrates.

The Babylon that Herodotus describes is mostly that created by Nebuchadnezzar, who extensively rebuilt the city. It was the largest city in the world, covering 2500 acres. The eastern part of the city was much the larger of the two, and contained the Esagila, the great temple of Marduk, with its associated ziggurat Etemananki. This latter was the building later popularly known as the Tower of Babel. It was three hundred feet high, and its uppermost storey was a temple clad in blue-glazed tiles. There were quays for trading vessels along the banks of the Euphrates, as it flowed through the city, and the river was spanned by a bridge on brick piles with stone capping, joining the east and west parts. The streets were laid out on a grid pattern. The city walls were double, as Herodotus describes them, and there was an outer triple rampart some miles away, the land between the outer rampart and the main walls being cultivated and irrigated by canals.

There is no evidence, apart from the Book of Daniel, that Nebuchadnezzar was mad for seven years, but he certainly ruled for many years, since he made an attempt to invade Egypt in 568–7 B.C., the thirty-seventh year of his reign. Nabonidus succeeded him in 556, but the exact manner of his doing so is uncertain. He was an Aramaean, born in Harran in the northern parts of Mesopotamia. It is not far from Edessa, and five hundred years later achieved some notoriety under the name of Carrhae, where Crassus was defeated and killed by the Parthians in 53 B.C. Nabonidus's mother was a priestess of Sin, the moon-god, in Harran. She brought her son to Babylon and found him office at court. She was a much-revered lady, living till the age of 102, when, in 547, she was taken back to Harran to be buried.

In Babylon, Marduk was the chief god, and the priests of Marduk were the most powerful faction, until the arrival of Nabonidus. Marduk was usually called simply "Bel", meaning "lord": originally he was probably a god of thunderstorms. His consort was Zarpanit, She Who Created Seed. His star was Jupiter, and his favourite beasts were horses, dogs and a dragon with a forked tongue. Nabonidus's close association with the moon-god led to the crystallization around him of the opposition to the priests of Marduk and his selection as king. Excavations in Babylon have led to the discovery of fragments of poems expressing propaganda for and against Nabonidus; it was no doubt a period filled with dissension.

His reign was naturally an uneasy one. There was strong opposition to his reign at home, and abroad he was conscious that Babylonia, a long, thin state stretching up the flatlands of the Tigris and Euphrates from the Persian Gulf, was strategically ill-designed to meet attack by any strong power. In 552, four years after coming to the throne, he left his realm to organize an Arabian province to defend one of his exposed flanks, leaving behind his son Belshazzar as viceroy.

He may also have left behind his wife Nitocris, to busy herself with her embankments and lakes outside the city and bridges within it, while her eldest son Belshazzar got on with the business of governing. Nitocris may have been a daughter of Nebuchadnezzar, and her marriage to Nabonidus may have led to his elevation to the throne, but this can be little but an excursion into guesswork.

During Nabonidus's absence his realm, whether or not as a result of Belshazzar's administration, was plagued by famine and economic difficulties. In 550 B.C., the sixth year of Nabonidus's reign, a momentous event occurred: the overthrow of the Median king by Cyrus the Persian. Within three years Cyrus had consolidated his power and was expanding his empire westwards with his attack on Lydia. The priests of Marduk in Babylon saw here a rising power that might restore them to the position they had lost with the coming of Nabonidus, disciple of the moon-god.

Nabonidus returned to Babylon in 542. Belshazzar had defended his frontiers, but internally his position was difficult. Nabonidus antagonized the priests of Marduk still further by starting the construction of a temple to Sin, the moon-god. The priests of Marduk offered Cyrus the surrender of Babylon in return for the restoration of their privileges. He invaded Babylonia from the north in 539; the campaign was a swift one, and the old Babylonian chronicle sums it up in terse brevity: "In the month of Tashritu Cyrus attacked the army of Akkad in Opis on the Tigris . . . on the fourteenth Sippar (inside the Median Wall) was seized without battle . . . Nabonidus fled . . . on the sixteenth day . . . the army of Cyrus entered Babylon without battle . . . afterwards Nabonidus was seized in Babylon when he returned there."

Herodotus enlarges this, and gives details of the fall of Babylon to Cyrus. The Babylonians, having met Cyrus in battle outside the city, were defeated and had to retire into the city. There, however, they had accumulated a large store of provisions and expected to be able to withstand a long siege. It appears that in the view of Herodotus's informants, the opposition within the city cannot have been strong enough to lead to its instant surrender, since Cyrus had to settle down to a long siege. After making no progress for some time, a plan for entering the city either occurred to Cyrus himself or was suggested to him by somebody else. He stationed troops at the point where the Euphrates flowed into the city and the point where it flowed out again, and took a force upstream to the place where Nitocris had excavated the lake. Here he had a canal dug to turn the Euphrates into the lake, which was by now a marsh. The water in the river sank so low that the Persians stationed at its entrance and exit were able to wade up it and enter the town. If the Babylonians had had any idea what Cyrus was doing they could have shut and barricaded the river-gates and, mounting the walls along the riverside, destroyed the Persian army in the trap they had entered; but the Persians took them completely by surprise. The Babylonians in fact told Herodotus that owing to the great size of the city the outer parts of it were captured by the Persian army without the people in the centre of the city knowing anything about it. There was some kind of festival in progress and they were still singing and dancing in the streets when the Persians appeared.

Nabonidus, returning to surrender to Cyrus, received a small principality in eastern Iran. There is a little confusion in the Book of Daniel between him and Nebuchadnezzar; the Nebuchadnezzar whose dream was interpreted to him by Daniel in chapter 4, and whom Daniel refers to as Belshazzar's father in 5.18, is Nabonidus.

Cyrus regarded himself as the liberator and protector of Babylon as much as its conqueror. One result of his conquest was the liberation of the Jews, some of whom had served as mercenaries in Nabonidus's Arabian venture, and their return to Jerusalem. Babylonia was, as Herodotus says, the richest province of his empire; in inscriptions in Akkadian, the ancient Semitic language used locally—Babylonian was a northern dialect of the language, Assyrian a southern—he proclaims himself as "Cyrus, king of the world, great king, legitimate

king, king of Babylon, king of Sumer and Akkad, king of the four
corners of the world". He installed his son Cambyses as viceroy in
Babylonia.

Despite this mild rule, discontent was widespread in Babylon, and
at the accession of the usurper Darius a pretender calling himself
Nebuchadnezzar III seized the throne there. His reign lasted less than
three months, but there was another uprising in the following year,
521, which Darius came in person to put down. According to Herodotus, the men of Babylon had taken exceptional measures to prolong
their resistance in the expected siege by reducing the consumption of
food. They herded all the women of the city together and strangled
them, each man keeping back from the general massacre only his
mother and one woman of his household to bake his bread for him.
Darius marched on the city and besieged it, but after twenty months
had failed to take it. A noble Persian called Zopyrus, son of one of
those fellow-conspirators who had helped Darius to seize the throne,
came to him with a plan: he mutilated himself and fled to the city,
pretending to be a deserter who had been caught and punished by
Darius. After persuading the Babylonians to give him the command
of some troops, and gaining their confidence by annihilating, by
previous arrangement with Darius, certain bodies of half-armed
troops that Darius sent forward to exposed positions, he was given
a high command. He used his position to order all the Babylonian
troops to mount the walls during a general assault, while he himself
opened the gates.

Darius treated Babylon much more severely than Cyrus had done.
He destroyed the inner city wall, pulled down the gates and had
three thousand of the leading citizens impaled. The rest he allowed to
go on living in the city and, since they had strangled so many of their
own women, he ordered the surrounding nations to send fifty
thousand women of their own people to Babylon. From these the
Babylonians of Herodotus's time were descended.

Darius rewarded Zopyrus with the governorship of Babylon, the
city he had been instrumental in ruining. Zopyrus's son was Megaby-
zus, who commanded the Persians against the Athenians who invaded
Egypt; but his grandson, another Zopyrus, deserted from the Persian
army and fled to Athens.

Discontent in Babylon bubbled on during Darius's long reign,
occasioned partly by burdensome taxation and the grievances of the
priests of Marduk. On the accession of Xerxes in 486 insurrections
became almost continuous, and after the latest of these in 482 Xerxes
took strong measures, demolishing much of the fortifications, in-
flicting extensive damage and desecration on the temple of Marduk

and the Tower of Babel, executing many priests and melting down the golden statue of Marduk.

At the time of Herodotus's visit about thirty years later, despite these depredations, Babylon was still a great and splendid city, its commerce flourishing and its wealth immense. The old Akkadian language had largely given way to Aramaic owing to the influx of strangers, including, perhaps, those fifty thousand women who had replaced the ones done away with before the siege. Numerous Iranians were settled there, engaged in commerce—excavators have turned up, among other things, the clay-tablet archives of Murashu and Son of Nippur, export-import dealers of the fifth century B.C.— and there were many Jews, but business was still largely in the hands of Babylonians and Aramaeans. Poets and astronomers were hard at work, the latter principally concerned with calculating the course of the moon and the planets.

The city was still supreme among other cities in size and importance a hundred years later, when Alexander embarked on his conquest of the world. Intending to make it his imperial capital, he restored the temple of Marduk, rebuilt the Tower of Babel, and recognized Marduk as the equal of Zeus. His plans came to nothing, since he died of a fever in Nebuchadnezzar's palace in 323. It was not until 275 B.C. with the foundation of Seleucia on the Tigris and the transfer there of part of the population of Babylon, that the decline of the great city really began: a decline that was so total that for most of the past two thousand years Babylon has been nothing but a group of mounds in a marshy plain.

THE SOUTH: EGYPT

V

The approach to Egypt——the delta——Herodotus enquires about the sources of the
Nile——visits Naucratis——famous prostitutes of Naucratis——first impressions
of Egypt——mummification, details of methods used——the Egyptians excessively
religious——Buto, city of the cobra-goddess——the marsh-Egyptians, their lives and
customs——how Herodotus believes the Greeks learned the names of the gods from
Egypt——city of Bast, the cat-goddess——burial-place of mummified cats——
Heliopolis——Memphis——Lake Moeris——the crocodile——Herodotus travels
rapidly south——hearsay accounts of what lies beyond——journey to Meroë——
appearance and customs of the Ethiopians——travels to Mendes——Tanis——
Pelusium——views the desert battlefield——visit to Cyrene——the tribes further
west——his hearsay stories of little value——Mount Atlas——the waterless desert to
the south——animals of the nomads' country——returns home to Halicarnassus.

SOME TIME AFTER 449 B.C. and before 446 the ship on which Herodotus was travelling approached the shores of Egypt from the north. He
was between thirty-five and thirty-eight years of age.

When they were still a day's sail from the shore, someone standing
in the bows hove the lead. The bottom was muddy, and the depth was
already as little as eleven fathoms, or sixty-six feet; which showed, as
Herodotus comments, how far out to sea the silt brought down by the
Nile extended.

The coastline, from the extreme west to the extreme east of the
cultivated land, he reckoned at 420 miles; an unusual error. It is about
150. The distance from the coast to Heliopolis, inland, where the
cultivated land narrowed to a few miles in width, is about forty miles
less. Thus Lower Egypt, the Nile delta, formed an inverted triangle
with its baseline on the coast to the north, and its apex at Heliopolis
in the south, Heliopolis being more or less on the outskirts of the
modern Cairo, not more than six miles from its centre and hard by the
airport.

All this triangle of country was broad and flat, with many swamps and
much mud. Herodotus was of the opinion—and the priests he spoke
to bore him out in this—that the whole fertile triangle of Lower
Egypt was built up by silt from the Nile. He also speculated that the
whole of the Nile valley might once, long ago, have been a gulf
similar to the Red Sea, which in the course of centuries had been
turned into dry land by the deposits of silt by the river. In this speculation he goes rather further than the facts available to him warranted,
but his general conclusion is undeniably true, that the Egypt to which
a traveller like himself sailed was, as he put it, a gift of the river, and
one that had only come into the possession of its inhabitants in com-
paratively recent times, geologically speaking.

He cites supporting evidence for his theory of the origin of Lower Egypt. For instance, the Nile delta projects into the sea beyond the line of the coast east and west of it; besides this, he had seen sea-shells on the hills, and had observed how salt exuded from the soil, even far off upstream in the neighbourhood of the pyramids. It was only above Memphis—in the narrows of Upper Egypt, twenty miles upstream from Heliopolis—that one began to find sand on the hills. Moreover, the soil of Egypt did not at all resemble that of Libya, which was reddish and sandy, or of Arabia and Syria, which consisted to a much greater extent of stone and clay. It was black and friable, as would be expected of an alluvial soil carried down by the river from distant Ethiopia. A competent scientist was lost in Herodotus: he had the knack—rarer than it might be, even in scientists—of looking at things with an eye unclouded by prejudices or preconceived notions, and bringing a drily detached mind to bear on what he saw.

The priests gave him another striking piece of evidence from Egyptian history. This was, that in the reign of Moeris—the Twelfth-Dynasty Pharaoh Ammenemes III, who reigned from 1842 to 1797 B.C.—the whole area below Memphis used to be flooded when the river rose twelve feet. This, he was told, was less than nine hundred years previously, though in fact it was about thirteen centuries and a half. Now, however, it flooded only if the river rose twenty-three and a half to twenty-four feet.

His informants, at this early stage of his Egyptian tour, were both shocked and sympathetic to learn from him that his own country, instead of being watered, like Egypt, by regular annual flooding, had to depend on rainfall to moisten the soil and cause the crops to grow. Clearly the Greeks would all starve one day when God chose to withhold the rain which at present it was his whim to send them at such moments as he chose. In Herodotus's view, however, the Egyptians were even worse off, since if the land in the fertile delta below Memphis continued to rise at the same rate, the day would come when the Nile's waters would no longer overflow and flood the fields. The Egyptians would then starve even more certainly than the Greeks, since they had no rainfall to fall back on.

For the time being, though, the farmers of Lower Egypt got their harvest with less trouble than any other people in the world. They did not need to cultivate the ground with plough or hoe; they merely waited for the river to rise and flood their fields, and as soon as the waters receded all they had to do was to sow the seed, turn their pigs loose to tread it in, wait for the corn to grow, harvest it, use the aid of the pigs again to thresh it, and put it in store.

The Nile divided, as Herodotus observed—there have been

changes over the centuries—into three major streams, below the town of Cercasorus, and ran to various mouths, that of Pelusium in the east and that of Canopus in the west, with a central stream running due north from the tip of the delta between them and reaching the sea at the Sebennytic mouth. There were other branches from the Sebennytic channel, the Saitic and the Mendesian, besides two channels which were not natural but excavated, running to the Bolbitic and Bucolic mouths.

Above Heliopolis, Upper Egypt narrowed to a fertile strip between mountain ranges, the Libyan on the west and the Arabian on the east: but after four days' voyage up the river from Heliopolis it broadened out again, until it reached Thebes, about nine days' journey from Heliopolis, or about 720 miles from the sea.

No one could tell Herodotus anything at all about the sources of the Nile, except for one person. This was the scribe who looked after the list of the treasures of Athena in the city of Sais in the delta—its ruins still stand at Sa el Hagar, on the main western, Rashîd or Rosetta branch of the Nile. He said that between Thebes and Elephantine there were two conical mountains called Crophi and Mophi, and that the Nile sprang up between them from springs of incalculable depth. The bottomless nature of the springs had been proved by the Egyptian king Psammetichus, the founder of the Twenty-sixth Dynasty—a man of Sais, like the scribe—who reigned from 664 to 610 B.C. Psammetichus had a rope made, many thousands of fathoms long, and let it down into the springs without reaching the bottom. The Nile, having issued from these springs, then flowed in two directions, half of it northwards and half of it southwards.

Herodotus thought, justifiably, that this account was hardly to be taken seriously. He later sailed up from Thebes to Elephantine and saw no evidence that the Nile's flow was against him for the first half of the journey and with him for the second. As for the bottomless spring, if Psammetichus did let his long plumb-line down a spring in that neighbourhood Herodotus thought it was more likely that the impact of the mountain through which the Nile flowed in that stretch of its course caused whirlpools and eddies in the water, and that it was these that prevented the plumb-line from reaching the bottom.

A major reason for his curiosity about where the Nile rose was that he thought it might solve the even greater problem of what it was that made the Nile behave as it did, unlike all other rivers, and rise to its annual flood in the summer months.

Various Greeks, whom he does not name, had put forward theories to account for this behaviour. One theory was that north winds in the summer held back the northward flow of the water and caused it to

pile up on itself. Herodotus dismisses this on the grounds that the
wind often failed to blow from the north in summer, but the Nile
flooded all the same; moreover, other rivers in North Africa which
ran in the same direction were not affected in the same way.

Another theory was, as he puts it, of a more legendary character.
It held that the Nile behaved as it did because it flowed from Ocean,
the great stream that according to some cartographers of those days
flowed round the known world. Herodotus remarks that he knows
of no river called Ocean, and in his opinion Homer, or some even
earlier poet, invented both the concept and the name. The theory
was based on a fairy-tale and it was impossible to prove it or disprove
it by rational argument.

The third theory he thought the most plausible, but at the same
time the furthest from the truth. This was, that the water of the Nile
came from snow, melting in the summer. Herodotus's habitual
scepticism here leads him astray, as scepticism sometimes will: since
he sees only the obvious impossibility of the explanation. His grounds
for denying its possibility are sensible enough. The Nile flows from
Libya through Ethiopia into Egypt—that is, from a very hot climate
towards one somewhat less hot. How, then, could there possibly be
snow at its source? He has plenty of evidence for believing that the
country to the south, in which the Nile rises, is extremely hot. In the
first place, the south wind blowing from those regions is a hot wind.
In the second, if there were snow in that part of the world there
would be rain, too; but rain does not fall in Egypt, except in the
regions immediately adjacent to the coast; and it is hardly to be
supposed that if no rain falls as you go south into Egypt, it will start
falling again if you go further south still. Thirdly, the people who
come from those regions are black, and it is the hot climate that makes
them black. Fourthly, cranes migrate there from Scythia and the north
in winter, to escape from the cold to a hot climate. It is clear, then,
that there can be no snow to the south, since if there were, none of
these things would be as they are. It stands to reason; and once
something stands to reason, the smell of dogma is hanging around in
the air somewhere.

Herodotus has a theory of his own, which he puts forward in a
slightly offhand manner, not perhaps out of modesty, but out of a
secret realization, which he is unwilling to admit even to himself,
that it is much less convincing even than the other three. It is, that as
a result of the violent storms of winter in more northerly latitudes the
sun is driven out of its course southwards towards the further parts
of Libya (by which term he means Africa). The sun, standing directly
above Libya, draws up most of the water from the streams and rivers,

so that in the winter months there is less water to feed the sources of the Nile. When the sun regains its more northerly course, it draws up moisture from all rivers equally and not only from the Nile. The result is that while all the other rivers are in flood during the winter, the Nile is much lower in winter than in summer because the waters that feed it are being dried up.

It is a theory that has that wonderful ingenuity typical of incorrect scientific theories. The operations of Nature are usually of a remarkable straightforwardness and simplicity, and it is almost invariably true to say that when this kind of weird complexity creeps in to explain a natural phenomenon, error creeps in with it.

The truth that baffled Herodotus baffled everyone else until about a century ago. In March and April the moisture-laden winds of the South Atlantic discharge their contents on to the highlands of the Lake Plateau that surrounds Lake Victoria, and on to the mountains of Ethiopia, the sources respectively of the White Nile and the Blue Nile. Lake Victoria and Lake Albert act as reservoirs for the head-waters of the White Nile, steadying its flow in the period of spate, and as the floodwaters proceed northwards they are further delayed by the swamps of the Sudd. At Khartoum the White Nile is joined by the Blue Nile, which has no such natural impediments. By June its waters are already swollen by the rains of Ethiopia, and by August the joint rivers are in full spate. In September the floodwaters reach Egypt, causing the annual inundations. In the late autumn the flood of the Blue Nile dies away; the steady flow of the White Nile maintains the winter river in its course through Egypt to the sea.

When the Nile overflowed, Herodotus says, the whole of Lower Egypt was changed into a great sea. The towns, remaining visible above the water, reminded him of the islands in the Aegean. He does not say where he first landed in Egypt, but it seems most probable, for many reasons, that he landed at the Canopic mouth and sailed up-river to his first place of residence, Naucratis.

In the season when the Nile was in flood, water transport was used not only along the Nile itself but all over the country, so that a traveller going from Naucratis to Memphis did not need to follow the bends of the river but could go straight across country. It was similarly possible to travel from the Canopic mouth not, as Herodotus did, by boat up-river, but across the flooded plain, passing the cities of Anthylla and Archandropolis on the way.

Anthylla was a city on the river, not far from the Canopic mouth. Ever since the Persian conquest its revenues had been devoted to keeping the wife of the reigning monarch in footwear. Archandropolis was further up the Canopic branch towards Cercasorus; its name was, as Herodotus says, Greek, and he thought it might be named after Archander, the mythical grandson of the mythical Achaeus, founder of the Achaean Greeks.

It was not surprising that in his first journey in Egypt he passed these places with Greek names, since Naucratis, his first destination, was a Greek city, a Milesian colony founded in 550 B.C. in the reign of Amasis (Amosis II) of the Twenty-sixth Dynasty, who reigned from 570 to 526 B.C. Amasis favoured the Greeks and granted them many privileges. Among these he presented them with the city of Naucratis to be used as a commercial headquarters for any Greeks who wished to settle in the country or visited it for purposes of trade. There was a colony there of Ionians and Dorians from various Asiatic Greek cities including Halicarnassus. Amasis also made grants of land to traders who did not wish to settle in Naucratis permanently, for them to build their temples on. The Halicarnassians and others had joined together to build the Hellenium, the largest and most frequented of the temples, on one of these tracts of land. The resident Asiatic Greek communities had the right to appoint the officers in charge of the river-port of Naucratis. Among other temples which had been built by Greek settlers and traders were the temples of Zeus, built by the Aeginetans; of Hera, built by the Samians, and of Apollo, built by the Milesians.

In the days of Amasis, Naucratis had been the only port available for foreign merchants in Egypt. If a merchant brought his ship into one of the other mouths of the Nile, because of a storm or from any other cause, he had to state on oath that he had done so only out of necessity and not by deliberate intent, and he was required to sail on as soon as possible to the Canopic mouth and Naucratis. If he was unable to do so owing to contrary winds he had to carry his goods to Naucratis by barge.

Amasis carried his good will to the Greeks so far as to contribute to the rebuilding of the temple of the Amphictyons at Delphi after it was burned down. He sent gifts to various other temples: a gold-plated statue of Athena and a painting of himself to Cyrene; two stone statues and a linen corslet to the temple of Athena at Lindos in Rhodes; and two wooden statues of himself to the temple of the goddess Hera in Samos, whose ruler Polycrates was a friend of his. These last, Herodotus says, were there during the time of his own exile in Samos. Amasis also married a Greek woman, Ladice, from Cyrene, and had the misfortune of being unable to consummate his marriage to her for some time. Finally he accused her of witchcraft, and told her that unless she lifted the spell before his next attempt she would be put to death. Ladice, having failed to convince Amasis that the charge was untrue, vowed secretly to present a statue to the temple of the goddess Aphrodite at Cyrene if on this final occasion the marriage could be consummated. The goddess answered her prayers, Amasis was success-ful at his next attempt and thereafter and came to love Ladice deeply, and Ladice had the statue of Aphrodite made and sent it to Cyrene, where, Herodotus says, it was still to be seen in his own time, looking outwards from the city. Amasis died a natural death before the Persian invasion, but when Cambyses, the Persian conqueror, learned who Ladice was he sent her back to her native Cyrene to live there in retirement.

Naucratis had one unusual claim to fame in that it had been the home of some particularly attractive prostitutes. The most famous was Rhodopis, a Thracian, who was born a slave in the household of a Samian, Iadmon. Aesop, the writer of fables, was a fellow-slave of hers: when Iadmon freed him he visited Croesus of Lydia and, being sent by Croesus on a mission to Delphi, so annoyed the citizens in some dispute that they threw him over a precipice. There is no confirmation of his reputed ugliness in Herodotus or any other writer of antiquity; it appears to have been an invention of the fourteenth century.

Rhodopis was brought to Egypt, and to Naucratis, by Xanthus, another Samian, in the time of Amasis, to follow her trade there. She did so, for her owner's profit, but her beauty so impressed a visitor from Mytilene, Charaxus, brother of the poetess Sappho, that he bought her freedom for a large sum of money. For this, on his return to Mytilene, Sappho lampooned him in one of her poems. Rhodopis remained in Naucratis and, following her trade now for her own profit, amassed a considerable fortune. In gratitude to the gods for her deliverance from servitude she spent a tenth of her fortune on as many roasting-spits as the money would buy, and sent them to the temple at Delphi, where Herodotus saw them himself, lying in a heap behind the altar dedicated by the people of Chios.

Another famous prostitute of Naucratis was Archidice, of whom we know nothing except that she was also beautiful, practised in Naucratis at a period later than Rhodopis, and was less gossiped about than Rhodopis but more widely known, since poems written about her circulated all over Greece.

During his stay at Naucratis Herodotus began to form his impres-sions of the country and of the people among whom he was living. The country, as he said, contained more monuments which defied description than anywhere else in the world. Everything about Egypt was remarkable: the climate was unlike any other climate, and the behaviour of the Nile was different from that of any other river. This being so, it was not surprising that the manners and customs of the Egyptians seemed to be in some way topsy-turvy, a reversal of whatever would be normal elsewhere.

So, the women went to market and saw to matters of trade, while the men stayed at home. Men carried loads on their heads, women carried them on their backs; women passed water standing up, men sitting down. Both men and women went indoors to relieve themselves, but went outside to eat, the reasoning behind this practice—stranger to Herodotus than to us—being that what was unseemly, though necessary, should be done in private, but what was seemly should be done openly. Sons were under no obligation to help their parents, but daughters were obliged to support them, whether they wished to or not.

There were no priestesses, men acting as priests of both goddesses and gods. Priests in other countries grew their hair long, but in Egypt they shaved their heads. In other countries relatives of the dead cut their hair off as a sign of mourning, but in Egypt, where men normally shaved their chins, they showed their respect for the dead by growing their hair long and allowing their beards to sprout. In weaving, other nations worked the weft upwards, the Egyptians worked it downwards. The Egyptians lived closely together with their animals, where other nations kept themselves apart from them. They used their feet to knead dough and their hands to knead clay; they even handled dung. They practised circumcision, while other nations—except those that had learned the practice from the Egyptians —left themselves as nature intended them to be. Egyptian men wore two garments each, women only one. At sea, the ring-bolts to which the sheets and halyards were made fast were fitted inboard instead of outboard. They wrote from right to left instead of from left to right.

For certain of their customs Herodotus had a guarded approval. The brazen cups from which they drank were scoured every day. Their clothes, which were made of linen—it was contrary to their religion to wear wool in a temple, or to be buried in wool—were washed most frequently. Even circumcision, which Herodotus looked on with disfavour, he admitted was practised by the Egyptians for the sake of hygiene, cleanliness being preferred to sightliness.

He was impressed by the assiduity with which the educated classes devoted themselves to preserving records of the past, and considered that in this respect the Egyptians were the most learned of all the peoples he had encountered. He thought them also the healthiest people in the world, after the Libyans, possibly as a result of their

Herodotus's Journey South to Egypt and Africa

A Theban scribe wild-fowling.

Gebel el-Tayr, the Bird mountain, near the entrance to El-Faiyûm in Egypt which Herodotus passed n his southern travels through Egypt.

custom of purging themselves for three days every month with emetics and clysters, which they did in the belief that all diseases came from the food a person ate; but Herodotus thought the principal cause of their good health was the constancy of the climate, since change, particularly change in the weather, was the prime cause of disease.

They ate loaves made from spelt, an inferior kind of grain, and drank wine made from barley, since they had no grapes. Some kinds of fish were eaten raw, after being either dried in the sun or salted. Quails, ducks and some small birds were eaten raw after being pickled in brine, but other kinds of birds, and fish, were either roasted or boiled.

It was the custom for young men to step aside to make room for older men in the street, and to get up from their seats when an older man came into the room: a custom, Herodotus says, resembling that of the Spartans. On meeting each other in the street they did not greet each other by name, but made a low bow, dropping one hand to the knee. As for dress, the men wore a linen tunic with a fringe hanging down round the legs, and a white woollen garment on top of this.

The practice of medicine was as strange as everything else in Egypt, since each doctor was responsible only for the treatment of one particular part of the body. So there were countless doctors, some concerning themselves with diseases of the eyes, others with the head, others with the teeth, the stomach and so on; while another doctor dealt with the diseases which could not be localized in any particular part of the body.

For all their robust health and length of life, the Egyptians were, like Webster in Eliot's poem, much possessed by death. Even at a party, when the meal was finished, a man would come in and carry round among the guests a wooden model of a corpse in a coffin, eighteen inches to three feet long, carved and painted to look as real as possible. This he would show to each guest in turn, saying: "Look on this body as you drink and enjoy yourself, for this is what you will look like when you are dead."

When a leading citizen died, all the women of the household plastered their faces with mud and went round the town together with the female relatives of the dead man, similarly besmeared, beating their bared breasts, while the men, in parties of their own, did the same. When this ceremonial was over they took the body to be mummified.

Mummification was a skilled profession, and the relatives as automatically took the body to the embalmers as, in modern times they would call in the undertaker. The embalmers would give them a quotation for the various grades of mummification, and show them specimens of the kind of work they did, the specimens being made of wood and painted in a natural and lifelike fashion. The best and most expensive process produced a mummy of such high perfection that it was supposed to resemble the god Osiris, whom Herodotus is always nervous of mentioning because he supposes Osiris to be the Egyptian equivalent of the Greek Dionysus, and there were certain mysteries of Dionysus that he always preferred not to talk about. The second grade of mummy was inferior to the first, and cheaper, and the third cheaper still. The embalmers would point out these differences in quality to the relatives, and when the relatives had decided which one they wanted and a price had been agreed on the embalmers would set to work on the body.

For the first grade of mummification, the brain was extracted through the nostrils with an iron hook, anything left of it in the cranial cavity being washed out "with drugs", as Herodotus puts it, the drugs being, no doubt, sterilizing fluids of some kind. An incision was then made in the flank with a flint knife and the contents of the abdomen extracted. The cavity was thoroughly cleansed and washed out first with palm wine and then with an infusion of powdered spices. It was then filled with a mixture of aromatic substances including crushed myrrh and cassia, but omitting frankincense. The body was then sewn up again and immersed for a period of exactly seventy days in what Herodotus calls natrum, which was a kind of brine, but one containing a naturally occurring mixture of sodium carbonate and sodium bicarbonate. At the end of the seventy days the body was washed and wrapped from head to foot in linen strips coated on the inner side with gum. In this condition it was returned to the relatives, who placed it in a wooden mummy-case shaped like the human figure. The case was sealed up and the mummy stored, standing upright against the wall, in a burial chamber.

The second grade of mummification omitted several of these steps. No incision was made, and the internal organs were not removed. Instead, oil of cedar was injected into the body through the anus, using a syringe, and the anus was stopped up to prevent the oil from escaping. The body was then pickled in natrum for the usual seventy-day period, and on removing it the oil was drained out. It is clear that what Herodotus refers to as oil of cedar was rather more than that, and must have possessed ingredients known only to the embalming profession. Its action was so powerful that it brought out all the organs, reduced to a liquid state, and since the super-brine had dissolved all the flesh nothing was left but bones and skin, and in this condition it was returned to the relatives. The third grade of mummification was more basic still.

In fact there were many more grades of mummification than Herodotus describes, and in mummies of the second class, for instance, incisions might be made; they have even been found in mummies of a very inferior quality. There must have been an opportunity for prolonged negotiations, the embalmers respectfully suggesting this or that, and the relatives debating among themselves just how far the purse could be stretched for the loved one, without overdoing it.

The body of any particularly beautiful woman, or one who was well known or had been the wife of a well-known man, was not given to the embalmers until three or four days had elapsed after death, to prevent violation of the corpse. If anyone—either an Egyptian or a foreigner—was drowned in the river or killed by a crocodile, the people of the nearest town were required by law to have the body mummified in the most expensive fashion and buried in a consecrated burial chamber. Relatives and friends were forbidden to touch it, the only people allowed to handle it being the priests of the Nile.

The custom of taking wooden representations of corpses round at social gatherings may or may not have been as universal as Herodotus makes it out to be—possibly he went to some exceptionally gloomy parties in Naucratis—but it cannot be denied that a kind of pervasive necrolatry hung over the ancient Egyptian scene. It is oppressive even at this distance of time, and to a life-loving Greek like Herodotus seeing it at close quarters it must have seemed particularly so. His only comment on it, however, is that the people of Egypt were excessively religious, more so than any other nation in the world. He was of the opinion that they were the first people to believe in the immortality of the soul. There are, of course, many variations in this belief, and according to Herodotus's account the one favoured by the Egyptians was that of the transmigration of souls. They believed that on death the soul entered into the body of another creature at the moment of that creature's birth. Having made the round of all living things, animals, birds and fish, it finally passed once again into the body of a man, the whole cycle occupying a period of three thousand years.

Religion in Egypt was a phenomenon of extreme complexity and subtlety, and Herodotus, for all his avid curiosity and his real talent for shedding some of his own set of ideas and prejudices in order to fathom the ideas and prejudices of others, was in no position to explore beyond its most superficial aspects. In Scythia he had been a little of a tourist but more of a traveller. He had little real contact with the people of the country, since he did not live with them and did not speak their language, but at least the people he did live with— the Greek traders of the Black Sea—knew them, and came into close contact with them, since the transactions of their calling demanded it. Moreover, there were few tourists in Scythia; it might even be said that there were none, or that if there were Herodotus was the first, and possibly the last.

Egypt, on the other hand, had known many Greek tourists, and Herodotus was one of them; an exceptionally curious and sympathetic tourist, but nevertheless more of a tourist than a traveller. The Egyptians he met were dragomans, interpreters, guides; the Greeks he lived with were traders, like the Greeks of Scythia, but they were much more remote from the intimate life of the country they lived in, since its people were conscious of their own ancient civilization and looked on the Greeks as barbarian upstarts. Besides, they had by now known many Greeks, both residents and visitors, merchants and tourists. A native, encountering a friendly, curious and sympathetic foreigner for the first time, may on a sudden impulse tell him what he thinks about God. When he has met a few hundred he will maintain a polite reserve.

Egyptian religion was subtle and complex in part because it was so ancient. It had been going on for three thousand years, starting, no doubt, like any other religion, with the idea of some fertility god or goddess who had to be placated to make the animals multiply and the crops grow. It had gone on through all these long centuries increasing in subtlety and sophistication, but, again like any other religion, it had not discarded its original notions as worthless and outworn but had carried them, or fragmentary memories of them, along with it. It had taken on new gods without throwing away the old; it had taken on a multitude of local gods and made them part of the pantheon. The religion of simple men was a very different matter from that of learned men. Private religion, what an individual believed and what religious observances he practised, was very different from state or official religion. Official religion was the business of the priests in the great temples, which were not places where the ordinary citizen went to worship, but places where the priests went about performing the rites and rituals necessary for the propitiation of the unseen world. The king performed the ceremonies there that brought him into contact with the god, though except at the most important festivals a priest acted as his deputy. The ordinary citizen was only concerned because his own well-being depended on the king's well-being. The great festivals overflowed from the temples into the streets and the citizen participated in them with jollities and festivities bearing much the same relation to the worship of the god as plum pudding to Christmas.

Of all this Herodotus saw nothing, since he was in no position to.

The great temples were open to sightseers, and Herodotus went to see their grandeurs and their treasures as the tourist visits St Paul's or St Peter's. To learn anything of Egyptian religion would have needed months of study and cultivated Egyptian friends willing to instruct him, and Herodotus had neither.

He saw the surface of it, caught occasional glimpses of what went on inside it, through cracks in its surface, and recorded what he saw; often what he saw was coloured by his own subtle and complex Greek religion.

Priests, he observed, washed even more than the ordinary Egyptian, since they bathed in cold water twice a day and twice every night. They also shaved their bodies all over every other day, to guard against the presence of lice and other insect infestations which would interfere with their religious observances. They wore nothing but linen and their shoes were made from the papyrus plant, these two materials for dress and shoes being the only ones allowed to them.

However, the hardships, or at least the restrictions, of their lives were compensated for by certain advantages. For instance, they were supported by the state. Their food, supplied to them free, consisted of bread made from the sacred grain, with an ample supply of goose-meat and beef, and wine, presumably barley wine. They were forbidden to eat fish, and never ate beans, not because these were forbidden but because they thought them unclean; in fact, they could not even bear to look at them. The Egyptians never sowed beans, and if they found any growing wild it would not occur to them to eat them, either raw or cooked.

He discovered that of all the gods worshipped by the Egyptians, only Isis and Osiris were worshipped by all of them. Isis was the great mother, the goddess of the productive earth; Osiris was the god of the underworld and its dark powers, of the flooding Nile and of vegetation. Isis was also associated with the moon, Osiris with the sun, though there were other more specific moon-gods and sun-gods. Nothing is simple in Egyptian religion; it is like poetry, a matter of overtones and undertones.

In the same way, different animals were sacrificed to the gods in different parts of Egypt, but bulls were sacrificed everywhere. They were considered to be the property of Apis, the bull-god of Memphis. A bull selected for sacrifice had to be exhaustively examined by the priests to make sure it had all the necessary qualities. If it passed all these tests it was marked for sacrifice by the priest, who twisted round its horns a band of papyrus which he sealed with wax and stamped it with his signet-ring. The penalty for anyone who sacrificed a bull not marked in this manner was death.

When the time for sacrifice came the bull was led up to the altar, where a fire was lighted. After a libation of wine had been poured, the bull was killed, its head cut off and its carcase flayed. The head served as a kind of scapegoat: those performing the sacrifice prayed that any disaster that threatened them, or their country, might be diverted and fall on the severed head of the animal. The head was then either sold to Greek traders, if there happened to be any at the market, or thrown into the river. This cutting off of the head and loading it with curses was practised with all sacrificial beasts, and was the reason why no Egyptian would use the head of any animal for food. The libation poured before a sacrifice was also a universal practice, as was the custom of fasting before the ceremony.

The carcase was treated in various ways according to which god was being worshipped. In sacrifices to Isis, after prayers had been said to the goddess the paunch was taken out of the carcase whole, leaving the intestines and fat inside the body. The legs, shoulders, neck and rump were cut off and the carcase stuffed with loaves of bread, honey, raisins, figs, frankincense, myrrh and other aromatic substances. Finally oil was poured over the carcase and it was burned. As it burned the worshippers beat their breasts, and afterwards they sat down and ate what was left over, which, as will be observed (though Herodotus, if he observed it, refrained from pointing it out), consisted of all the portions fit for eating, the revolting and the inedible being reserved for the god.

Bull-calves were also used for sacrifice, but cows never, since they were regarded as sacred to Isis. The Egyptians held the Greeks in great distaste for their habit of eating cows' meat, and for this reason no Egyptian would kiss a Greek, use a Greek knife, spit or cauldron, or even eat the flesh of a bull if it was known to have been killed or carved with a Greek knife.

As for bulls and cows that died a natural death, cows could be thrown into the river, but bulls were buried on the outskirts of the town with one horn—sometimes both—sticking out of the ground to mark the spot. After the carcase had been given time to rot, the bones were loaded into a barge and taken to a town called Atarbechis on the island of Prosopitis in a branch of the Nile between Naucratis and Sais. The town was known to the Greeks as Aphroditopolis. There was a temple there to Hathor, the cow-goddess, and it was from there that the barges travelled to all parts of the delta to collect the bones of cattle for burial.

Other animals were sacrificed, or not sacrificed, according to the locality. Egyptians living in the province of Thebes, or whose temple was dedicated to the Theban Amun—the great god of Thebes, some-

times identified with Re or Ra, the falcon-headed sun-god of Heliopolis, as Amun-Re—never sacrificed sheep, but only goats: since the
ram (as well as the goose) was sacred to Amun. Those, on the other
hand, who lived in the province of Mendes in the north-east of the
delta, near the Mendesian and Tanitic mouths, or who worshipped
the fish-goddess Hat-mehit of Mendes, never sacrificed goats but only
sheep.

Even in this simple rule there lurked a complication. The Thebans
did, in fact, sacrifice one ram a year, and, having skinned it,
wrapped the fleece round the statue of Amun, to commemorate the
occasion when, it was said, Amun wished to conceal himself from the
moon-god Khons (whom Herodotus considered to be the same
divine personage as Heracles) and adopted this means of doing so.
Those involved in sacrificing the ram then beat their breasts in mourning for its death and buried the remains in a consecrated sepulchre.

The pig was regarded as an unclean animal, associated with Set,
the god of storms and violence, brother and murderer of Osiris.
Anyone accidentally touching a pig would immediately plunge into
the river, fully clad, to cleanse himself. Swineherds were the lowest
class of people and, though pure Egyptians, were the only people in
the country never to enter a temple. They did not even intermarry
with the rest of the community, but looked for wives only among the
daughters of other swineherds.

Nevertheless, pigs were sacrificed to the Moon and to Osiris. To
both they sacrificed pigs on the day of the full moon, and afterwards
ate the flesh. When sacrificing to the Moon-god Khons (represented
as a man), after the pig had been slaughtered the least edible parts—
the tip of the tail, the spleen, and other undesirable elements—were
put together with all the belly-fat and burned, while the edible meat
was eaten by the worshippers on the same day, that of the full moon;
they would on no account eat pig's meat at any other time. Poor people
who could not afford pigs would make model pigs out of dough, bake
them and offer them for sacrifice in place of real ones.

When sacrificing to Osiris—whom Herodotus calls Dionysus—a
pig was procured from a swineherd, slaughtered before the door of
the house, and given back to the swineherd to be taken away.

Bulls, bull-calves, sheep, goats, pigs and geese were the only animals
sacrificed by the Egyptians, according to Herodotus, and all had first
to pass the priests' tests for "cleanliness".

All animals, wild and tame, were regarded as sacred. Some were
kept in captivity by hereditary guardians, as representing the gods to
whom they were sacred—rams and geese to Amun, asses, okapis and
hippopotamuses to Set, apes and ibises to Thoth, and so on—and

persons praying to the gods before them would reward the keeper by shaving some of the hair off their children's heads and giving an equivalent weight of silver to the keeper, who would devote all or some of it to feeding-stuffs for the animals in his charge.

The deliberate killing of a sacred animal was punishable by death; for accidental killing the penalty was whatever the priests decided. But for killing an ibis, either accidentally or deliberately, the punishment was inevitably death.

Wild animals included the crocodile, the hippopotamus, jackals, hares and apes; bears and wolves, both rare, according to Herodotus; and such denizens of the Nile and the marshes as otters, eels and frogs. Animals of the desert included gazelles, antelopes, lions, ostriches, ibexes and camels. Among birds there were vultures, eagles, flamingoes, geese—including one mysteriously referred to by Herodotus as the fox-goose—and the sacred ibis.

Cats and dogs were much beloved of their owners. When a cat died, all the residents of the house shaved their eyebrows; when a dog died, they shaved the whole body, including the head. Herodotus says that when a house caught fire none of the residents took any steps to put the fire out, being too intent on preventing the cats of the house from immolating themselves. They stood in a line, each one a little way from his neighbour, trying to keep away the cats, who nevertheless always succeeded in slipping through the line, or jumping over it, and hurling themselves into the flames, to the deep distress of the Egyptians. This seems one of the least convincing items of Herodotus's account of Egypt, though no less so than the odd behaviour of the female cats who, having once had kittens, avoided the toms; but the toms, deprived of their pleasure, stole the kittens and killed them, so that the cats, wanting more kittens, looked again among the toms for mates. But for this, Herodotus says, the number of domestic animals would be even greater than it was. It is never safe, after all the proofs of Herodotus's veracity despite the centuries of doubt, to accuse him of drawing the long bow, but even his most sincere admirer must suspect in his darker moments that in this matter of cats he goes a little far.

It is not difficult to tell which places in Egypt Herodotus visited but the order in which he visited them is less easy to determine. From Naucratis he may have gone to Sais or by a sea passage to Buto. It is certain from his description that he had the experience of approaching Buto from the sea. From Naucratis it would seem most natural that he should travel up-river to Sais, which lay, like Naucratis, on the Canopic, the most westerly, branch of the Nile. On the other hand, if he went first to Sais, it hardly seems possible that he would go a hundred miles round by sea when Buto was barely twenty miles away by land. The conclusion must be that he travelled from Naucratis downstream and round the coast to approach Buto, subsequently making an easy cross-country journey from there to Sais.

Buto he describes as a great city at the Sebennytic mouth of the Nile, on the right as one entered the river from the sea. Its ruins, near Shâba, stand now twelve miles from the nearest point of the coast, and even this is only the boundary of the swamps. The true sea, beyond the Bahra el Burullus, is twenty-five miles away. In the centuries not only have the courses of the Nile through the delta changed, the land has crept northwards, extending ever further into the Mediterranean.

Buto was the city of the cobra-goddess, the guardian spirit of Lower Egypt, whose image on the royal diadem was a protection for the king. She was the nurse of Horus the falcon-god and Bast the cat-goddess, children of Isis and Osiris. The city of Buto had been the capital of Lower Egypt before the unification of the kingdoms about 3100 B.C.

There were temples there to Apollo and Artemis—by whom Herodotus meant Horus and Bast—but the greatest was the shrine of Buto, whom Herodotus identifies with Leto, the mother of Apollo and Artemis by Zeus. This was an immense building with a gateway sixty feet high; but to Herodotus's eye the most remarkable thing about it was not its size or that of its gateway but a shrine within the enclosure made of a single block of stone, cubical in shape, each side being sixty feet in length. The roof of the temple was also, he says, formed of a single block of stone, which projected beyond the walls to a distance of six feet. The temple contained the oracle of Buto which, according to Herodotus, was held in greater repute than any other oracle in Egypt.

Divination was an important branch of religion in Egypt. Each day and each month were assigned to a particular deity, and it was possible from the date of a man's birth to determine his character and his fortune and foretell the date of his death. The Egyptians made a particular study of omens and prognostics, and kept a record of the effects of any unusual occurrence or manifestation, in the expectation that these would be duplicated on future occasions. The art of divination was a divine one, not to be practised by any man; prophecies were uttered by the oracles of the gods, particularly of Amun (Zeus), Horus (Apollo), Net (Athena), Bast (Artemis), Set (Ares), Khons (Heracles) and Buto, the most respected of all. Among its other noted achievements, the oracle of Buto had advised the son of the great Sesostris (by whom Herodotus means Ramesses II) how to recover from his blindness; it had told Mycerinus, long ago in the Fourth Dynasty, when he was going to die; and it had told Psammetichus how bronze men would come from the sea and deliver him from his enemies. It had also told the Persian king Cambyses that he would die at Ecbatana, which was comfortable news for him, since Ecbatana was his capital city and he confidently expected to die of old age there. However, according to Herodotus's story, while Cambyses was with his army in Syria he had the misfortune to wound himself with his sword in the thigh, in just the same spot where he had wounded Apis the sacred Egyptian bull in Memphis. It seemed to him that he had done himself a serious injury, and when he enquired what place this was it turned out that there was another Ecbatana in Syria, and this was it. Shortly gangrene set in and he duly died, in fulfilment of the prophecy.

After the temple of Buto, what most impressed Herodotus about the city was the island called Chemmis (there was a city of the same name in Upper Egypt). This was situated in a broad, deep lake near the temple, and according to Herodotus's Egyptian informants it was a floating island. This astonished him, and he wondered if there could actually be such a thing as an island that floated. He had to report, concerning this one, that he never saw it move, and nothing about its appearance suggested that it was floating.

There was a legend about it. When the goddess Buto, one of the eight original deities of Egypt, lived in the place named after her, she was in charge of Horus and Bast, the children of Isis and Osiris, and she succeeded in saving them from the wrath of Set, the god of storms and violence, by hiding them in this island; which, apparently, she could more effectively do if it floated. There was a large temple of Horus on the island with three separate altars, besides numerous date-palms and other trees.

Assemblies were held in honour of the goddess at Buto, as they were of the principal local deity at other cities. Herodotus gives no particular description of the one at Buto, though he does of those at Busiris, Bubastis and Papremis, from which it may be deduced that he was not at Buto when such a festival took place. He records, however, that any field-mice or hawks found dead in the delta were taken to Buto to be buried. This was because the goddess Buto was the guardian deity of these creatures. For a similar reason, cats which died were taken to Bubastis, where they were embalmed and buried in sacred receptacles; ibises were taken to Hermopolis—Hermopolis Magna, near the apex of the delta—which was a principal seat of the worship of Anubis the jackal-god, patron of embalmers and god of necropolises, besides being the burial-place of the sacred ibis. Dogs and weasels, however, were buried in the towns to which they belonged, though in sacred burial-places; whereas bears and wolves were buried wherever their corpses happened to be found.

At Buto Herodotus was in an excellent position to enquire into the lives and customs of the Egyptians who lived in the marsh-country nearest the sea. In most matters they followed the same way of life as other Egyptians, but there were a few peculiarities. They had, for instance, found ways of living at little expense on certain products of the water-lily or lotus. These grew in great profusion when the river was full and flooded the neighbouring flat-lands. The people gathered them and dried them in the sun, and picked out from the centre of each flower a seed resembling a poppy-head. These seeds they ground, making a kind of flour, which they baked into loaves. The root of the lotus was also edible; it was round, about the size of an apple, and sweet to the taste.

Another kind of lily found in the river resembled a rose in appearance. Its fruit was formed on a separate stalk from that which bore the blossom, and looked rather like a wasp's comb. This fruit contained several seeds each the size of an olive-stone, which were eaten either green, as picked, or dried.

Papyrus-reed was also eaten by the marsh-Egyptians. The reeds were pulled up and cut into two, the lower part—about eighteen inches in length—being eaten after baking in a closed pan heated to red heat.

Some of the marsh-Egyptians, however, lived on nothing but fish, which they ate after first gutting them and drying them in the sun.

They extracted oil from the castor-oil plant, which was prolific in its growth and had a disagreeable smell. The people sowed it along the banks of rivers and lakes. When the fruit was gathered it was either crushed in a press or boiled down. The oil so obtained was burned in lamps, though its smell was unpleasant.

The whole country was infested by swarms of gnats, and in the marsh-country, where they were at their worst, the people had nets which they used for fishing during the day and hung over and round their beds at night; but in the country south of the marshes it was sufficient protection to sleep on raised towers, since the winds prevented most of the gnats from rising to these heights.

From Buto Herodotus made his way to Sais on the east side of the Canopic branch of the Nile.

Two hundred years before his visit, Sais had been a centre of national revival after the defeat of the Nubian dynasty by the Assyrians. A local prince, Necho, had been captured by the Assyrian king Ashurbanipal, and carried off to Nineveh. Ashurbanipal decided Necho was a man he could get on with, and sent him back to Sais to be local ruler, at a time when the whole of Lower Egypt and much of Upper Egypt was in the hands of local rulers, nominees of the Assyrians: the period known to the Greeks as the Dodecarchy.

Necho's son Psammetichus, inheriting Sais from him, also inherited many troubles, since his fellow-princes of the delta suspected him, perhaps justifiably, of being over-ambitious. He sent for advice to the oracle at Buto, and received the reply that vengeance on his adversaries would be brought to him by bronze men from the sea. Not long afterwards a company of Ionian and Carian sea-raiders were forced by bad weather to land on the Egyptian coast, and proceeded to support themselves by their chosen profession of raiding and pillaging. They were wearing bronze armour, and an Egyptian who sighted them and got away, having never seen such a thing before, hastened to Psammetichus with the news that a company of bronze men was harrying the countryside. Psammetichus saw in this the fulfilment of the oracle, and persuaded the Greeks by generous offers of reward to enter his service. With their aid he defeated his enemies and united Lower Egypt under his own rule, becoming the first of the Twenty-sixth Dynasty or Saite kings.

His successor was Necho II, who did not, as Herodotus believes, begin the construction of a canal to the Red Sea from the Nile south of Bubastis; the canal existed already, but Necho had it widened so that instead of one, two triremes could go down it side by side. It was four days' journey from the Nile to the Red Sea by canal.

This work was not finished in Necho's time—its completion was left to Darius a hundred years later—but, having the Red Sea much on his mind, and being convinced that "Libya"—Africa—was "washed on all sides by the sea except where it joins Asia", as Herodotus puts it, Necho sent off a fleet of ships manned by Phoenicians from the Red Sea end of the canal, with orders to sail round Africa and return to Egypt via the Straits of Gibraltar and the Mediterranean. The Phoenicians sailed down the Red Sea into the Indian Ocean. In the autumn they put into whatever point of the African coast they had reached, prepared a patch of ground, sowed seed on it and waited for the harvest. Having got in the grain, they put to sea again. After two full years, and during the course of the third year, they passed the Pillars of Hercules—the Straits of Gibraltar—and so entered the Mediterranean and returned to Egypt.

On their return they stated that as they sailed on a westward course round the southern end of Africa, they had the sun on their right, that is, to the north of them. Herodotus says that he himself does not believe this statement, though it is up to others to believe it if they wish: another instance of his cautious and rational scepticism, which is so pronounced a characteristic of his that it is difficult to imagine his being fooled by some unlikely story about, say, cats.

Necho also campaigned in Palestine and Syria against the Babylonians, following their overthrow of the Assyrians, since their rule appeared to offer a threat to Egypt.

Josiah, the king of Judah, unwisely decided to take a hand in this struggle. As it says in the second book of Kings, 23: 29: "In his [Josiah's] days, Pharaoh-necoh king of Egypt went up against the king of Assyria to the river Euphrates." But then Necho, as it says in the second book of Chronicles, 35: 21, "sent ambassadors to him, saying, What have I to do with thee, thou king of Judah? I come not against thee this day, but against the house wherewith I have war; and God hath commanded me to make haste: forbear thee from meddling with God, who is with me, that he destroy thee not." Nevertheless, turning back to II Kings, "king Josiah went against him; and he slew him at Megiddo . . . and his servants carried him in a chariot dead from Megiddo, and brought him to Jerusalem, and buried him in his own sepulchre."

Necho's victory was short-lived, since he was defeated with great loss at Carchemish soon afterwards by the Babylonian Nebuchadnezzar.

Necho was succeeded by a second Psammetichus, and he by Apries. Apries followed an aggressive foreign policy, which in the end led to his being turned off his throne. He had sent an army against Sidon and fought a naval battle off Tyre, and finally came to grief at Cyrene.

Cyrene was a Greek colony on the north African coast said to have been founded by one Battus from the island of Thera in 631 B.C., some sixty years before the doom of Apries. Numerous Greek settlers came to join the colony in the succeeding years, and took over more of the surrounding countryside, until, in the time of the pharaoh Apries, the king of Libya, Adicran, decided to expel them, and sent to Apries for aid. Apries sent an army, but it was so severely defeated by the colonists—no doubt, as Herodotus says, because the Egyptians had never fought Greeks before and did not know the way of it— that few of his men returned home.

These few decided that Apries had deliberately sent his army to destruction, in order to render his people easier to rule. On returning home they joined together with the friends of those who had been killed and rebelled against Apries. Apries sent a functionary of his,

Amasis—a man from Siuph in the district of Sais—to try to persuade the rebels to submit, but the rebels, instead of submitting, offered Amasis the throne, and he thought it wisest to accept it.

Apries, hearing of this, sent another of his courtiers to command Amasis to return. Amasis, however, on receiving this summons, rose in his saddle and, breaking wind, told the envoy to take *that* back to his master. Apries was so infuriated by this reply that he had the envoy's nose and ears chopped off. This, in turn, infuriated the rest of the court so much that most of them went off to join the rebels.

Apries summoned his mercenaries, thirty thousand Carians and Ionians, and sallied forth to fight the Egyptians under Amasis. Apries was defeated and taken, a prisoner, to his former royal palace at Sais. Amasis, a genial and good-humoured man, treated him kindly, but his people objected to this, and demanded that Apries should be handed over to them. Amasis finally yielded: Apries was strangled and his body buried in the temple of Net at Sais, near the shrine, on the left-hand side as you go in, as Herodotus says; though he calls it the temple of Athena.

Amasis was that altogether rare and exceptional phenomenon, a light-hearted monarch. At first his subjects were a little contemptuous of him, being conscious of his very ordinary background and up-bringing. Among the treasures of his palace was a golden footbath that he and his guests used to wash their feet in, among other things. He had it melted down and turned into a statue of the god, which he set up in a prominent place in the town. After it had been treated for some time with proper reverence by all, he called the leading citizens together and made a short speech. He said this statue of the god had been a footbath, which they had not only washed their feet in but had also vomited and relieved themselves in whenever they felt like it. He himself was something like his footbath, in that he had been a very ordinary person, but now he was a king; and just as they had taken to revering his footbath after its transformation, it would be seemly if they treated him with similar respect after his.

He organized his working day according to his own individual views. He worked on the business of his kingdom from dawn till mid-morning. After that he spent the rest of the day in frivolous amusements, drinking and joking with friends. His advisers were shocked by this behaviour and recommended him to change his ways. His excessive levity, they said, did nothing to maintain his royal dignity. If he would only sit all day on his throne, attending to the affairs of his kingdom, the Egyptians would know that a great monarch ruled them, but his present conduct was not suitable for a king.

Amasis replied that archers, having used their bows to shoot with, unstrung them afterwards. If they left them always under tension they would be useless when they were needed. In the same way a man needed time for relaxation and enjoyment, since any man who was always serious and never permitted himself any amusement would either have a stroke or go mad. For this reason the wise man divided his time between duty and leisure.

It was said that before Amasis came to the throne he had had a similar approach to life, never overburdening himself with cares. When he was short of money to enjoy himself he would even go so far as to take things that did not belong to him, in order not to go short. He had several times been taken before the oracle on suspicion of theft. Sometimes the oracle had found him guilty, sometimes not. Now that he was pharaoh he had the greatest respect for those gods whose oracles had convicted him, saying they perceived the truth and were gods indeed; whereas those who had acquitted him he dismissed with contempt as worthless. He neglected their temples, contributed nothing to their treasuries and performed no sacrifices to them.

He reigned for forty-four years, and little is known of his reign except that he worked to promote and maintain good relations with all the neighbouring powers, markedly favoured the Greeks and Greek customs, married—among many others—Ladice of Cyrene, and devoted most of his energies to the domestic affairs of Egypt. The country knew an unexampled and unrepeated period of prosperity under his long reign, a good-natured, intelligent and reasonably amoral monarch being about the best fortune those who live under an absolute monarchy can hope for. Amasis was fortunate to the end, since he died shortly before the invasion of the Persians that established Cambyses on the throne of Egypt as the first of the Twenty-seventh, Persian Dynasty.

He introduced a measure that Solon learned from him and introduced to Athens. This was that every man, once a year, must declare before the governor of his province the source of his livelihood. Failure to do this, or to prove that the source was an honest one, was punishable by death.

The goddess of Sais was Net or Neith, whom the Greeks identified with Athena, the virgin daughter of Zeus and Metis, a harmonious blend of power and wisdom. Net was represented as a woman wearing a red crown, and bearing a shield with crossed arrows. She was a guardian of coffins and of the Canopic jars that contained the viscera of dead persons, Net's particular jar—there were always four—being the receptacle of the stomach.

Her temple at Sais was already enormous by the time Amasis came
to rule there. The walled temple enclosure measured about seven
hundred by three hundred yards, and its wall was about fifty feet high.
Amasis added to it what Herodotus describes as a "marvellous
gateway", far outrunning all others he saw in its size and magnificence.
These Egyptian gateways or propylaea consisted of a pair of obelisks
or truncated pyramids made of massive blocks of stone, the faces
inscribed with carved hieroglyphics. Amasis also contributed to the
temple some colossal statues and an avenue of man-sphinxes, and
carried out repairs to the main temple structure with immense blocks
of stone, some from the quarries near Memphis and the others—the
biggest—from Elephantine, at the site of the present Aswan Dam,
which was twenty days' voyage by river from Sais.

What astonished Herodotus most was a huge monolith thirty-five
feet long, twenty-three feet broad and thirteen feet high, which had
been hollowed out so that there was a room inside it measuring thirty
feet by twenty, and eight feet high: the walls, floor and ceiling of the
room being, in fact, made of a single mass of stone between one and a
half and two and a half feet thick.

This block had also been brought from Elephantine. It had taken
two thousand men, all of the seaman-navigator class, three years to
transport it to Sais. It was intended to be taken into the temple
enclosure, presumably to serve as a shrine, but in Herodotus's time
it was lying outside the entrance. There were various stories to account
for the abandonment of the plan to take it inside the temple. One was
that during the process of moving it the man in charge of the operation groaned so loudly at all the time and trouble it was taking that
Amasis, overhearing him, took this groan for a bad omen and ordered
the stone to be left lying where it was. Another version was that one
of the workmen who were levering it along with crowbars was
crushed to death below it, this again being taken as a bad omen.

The temple also contained a massive recumbent image—of whom,
Herodotus does not say—seventy-five feet long.

Of all this immense magnificence and the labour that created it very
little remains. The modern town of Sa el Hagar was built on top of the
ruins, since these formed an artificial mound which preserved it from
inundation during the floods.

Although the temple and city of Sais were much enlarged and
enriched in the period of the Saite kings, both were already ancient
long before the time of Amasis, who had been dead a mere eighty
years at the time of Herodotus's visit (he reigned from 570 to 526 B.C.).
Herodotus was able to visit, as well as the temple, the royal palace at
Sais, and the object that most interested him there was a wooden cow,

In Egypt Herodotus was fascinated by the presence of the exotic splendours, which were brought from all over Africa by slaves and tribute bearers. He often encountered such porters as these two Sudanic slaves bearing tropical fruits, ebony, plumes, ivory, gold, and a pet baboon. It was from men such as these that Herodotus' perennial accounts of the factual and fantastic marvels of the great African continent were collected.

hollow inside, and plated with gold, that stood in a richly decorated chamber of the palace. Incense burned before it all day, and a lamp was kept alight all night in the room. This cow dated from the time of Mycerinus (Menkaure), the son of Cheops and nephew of Cheops's successor Chephren. Mycerinus reigned two thousand years before Herodotus's time—about 2500 B.C.—and it was said that he had had the hollow cow made as a tomb for his daughter. Overcome by grief at her death—she was his only child—he wished to give her a tomb that was unlike any other. In a neighbouring room there were twenty or so naked wooden statues of enormous size. The priests told Herodotus these were statues of Mycerinus's concubines; he passes the information on but doubted whether it was true. Another story was that Mycerinus had conceived an unnatural passion for his daughter and violated her, which distressed her so much that she hanged herself. Her mother in her fury cut off the hands of all the servants who had connived at this outrage by allowing the king access to her daughter: and the statues in the neighbouring room represented these servants, as could be seen from the fact that they had no hands. Herodotus thought this story even less likely than the other. It was true that the statues had no hands, but the hands could plainly be seen lying on the ground near the feet of the statues, and it was obvious that they had merely dropped off through age.

The cow was covered with a purple cloth, leaving only the head and the neck exposed, these being plated with gold of considerable thickness. Between its horns there was a gold disc representing the sun. The cow, which was the size of a large living cow, was not standing but kneeling. At the festival held every year at which the Egyptians beat themselves in honour of Osiris—whose Greek equivalent, Dionysus, Herodotus as usual nervously refrains from naming—the cow was taken out from the chamber into the sunshine, since the story ran that on her deathbed Mycerinus's daughter had begged him to allow her once a year to see the sun. Since persons who hang themselves rarely have the opportunity to express wishes on their deathbeds, this hints at a third alternative story perhaps as improbable as the other two.

Mycerinus, after the death of his daughter, received a message from the famous oracle at Buto telling him that he was destined to live only six more years and would die during the seventh. He sent back a message to the oracle reproaching the god angrily for permitting a man so gentle, amiable and pious as himself to die so soon, when his father and uncle, who had closed the temples, neglected the gods and oppressed their subjects, had lived to a ripe old age. The oracle replied that his life was being shortened exactly for this reason; it was

E

destined that Egypt should suffer for a hundred and fifty years, and
while his father and uncle, Cheops and Chephren, had seen this and
collaborated in the infliction of suffering, Mycerinus had failed to do so.

Mycerinus, accepting his fate, dedicated himself thenceforth to a
life of pleasure, drinking with his companions every evening in rooms
brilliantly lit with innumerable lamps, so turning night into day in
order as far as possible to lengthen the six years that remained to him.
He travelled from place to place, visiting every particularly delightful
spot of which he had been told, so as to enjoy his pleasures in a setting
of woodland pools and glades. So, unable to defeat death, he cheated
it as far as lay in his power.

When Amasis died, shortly before the Persian invasion, his body
was mummified and buried in the temple of Net at Sais, in the sepulchre
he had had prepared there: but when Cambyses the Persian conqueror
arrived in Sais after his victory over the Egyptian forces, he had the
body of Amasis taken from its tomb and subjected to various indigni-
ties. It was lashed with whips and pricked with goads, and its hairs
were plucked out one by one. Finally it was burned, an offence to
both Persians and Egyptians, since the Persians believed that fire was
a god, and it was wrong to feed a man's dead body to him, while the
Egyptians believed that fire was a living creature, which should not
be allowed to eat dead bodies. The embalming of bodies was practised,
in part, so that they should not be eaten by worms or other animals.

While Herodotus was at Sais, he was able to attend the annual
festival in honour of the goddess Net, when sacrifices were made to
her. The night of the sacrifices was called the Festival of Lamps; it
was the custom for everyone to burn lamps in the open air round
their houses. The lamps were flat dishes filled with oil and salt, with
a floating wick, and continued to burn throughout the night. The
celebration was held throughout the country, and in all the cities as
well as Sais lamps were lit in the streets and gardens of the town on
this night of the festival of Net.

From Sais Herodotus travelled to the place he calls Papremis, which
is thought to have been Xois or Chois, a city on an island in the
Sebennytic branch of the Nile. The city was sacred to Set, the angry
god, murderer of Osiris. It seems to have been the capital of the
western delta in the time of the shadowy Fourteenth Dynasty, about
1600 B.C. According to Manetho, the priestly scribe of the time of
the first two Ptolemies—between 304 and 246 B.C.—who compiled
a list of all the pharaohs, no fewer than seventy-six rulers flourished
during this brief period, when the Hyksos, the Shepherd Kings from

Arabia, already ruled the eastern delta as the Fifteenth Dynasty. But little is known of these seventy-six Egyptians who ruled what must have been tiny fragments of Egypt in what is called the Second Intermediate Period. The Hyksos learned to worship Set, and adopted him as their national god, presumably since he was the nearest thing in the Egyptian pantheon to Baal. Many Egyptians in the north were devoted to the worship of Set, both before and after the time of the rough and savage Hyksos kings, but half a millennium afterwards, during the Twenty-first Dynasty, Set was overthrown by the pious triad of Thebes, Amun, Mut and Khons. Herodotus identifies Khons with Heracles, though whether he took Mut to resemble Alcmene, mother of Hercules, is less certain, since he makes no mention of her. Mut differed from Alcmene in certain particulars, such as being Amun's wife where Alcmene was Zeus's mistress, and moreover being originally a vulture-goddess.

Of more interest to Herodotus than the goddess Mut was the hippopotamus, which was held sacred in Papremis and the surrounding districts, though it was not sacred elsewhere. He describes it succinctly: an animal the size of a very large ox, with four legs, cloven hooves, a snub nose, a horse's mane and tail, conspicuous tusks and a voice like a horse's neigh. Its hide, he says, is so thick and tough that when it is dried it can be made into spear-shafts.

It seems that Herodotus spent only a little time in Papremis. It is clear that he visited it, since he saw there the skulls of the Persians who had been killed by the army of Inarus, the Libyan king who rose against the Persians in the time of Darius and was assisted for a time by the ill-fated Athenian expedition of 460 B.C. He remarks that the skulls were extraordinarily thin, like those of the Persian warriors he later saw on the older battlefield near the Pelusian mouth of the Nile. However, it seems that he cannot have been there during the annual festivities in honour of the god Set, since his description of these is based only on what he was told about them by the men of Papremis. Apparently, besides the usual rites and sacrifices such as were practised elsewhere, there was an organized battle or brawl at the entrance to the temple, typical of the worship of this violent god. His Greek equivalent was the brutish and noisy Ares, legitimate son of Zeus by his wife and sister Hera.

On the day before the festival the image of the god, in a small gold-plated wooden shrine, was taken to a different building some little distance away from the temple. As sunset approached on the day of the festival only a few of the priests continued to busy themselves about the image of Set in its temporary home. The rest took up their stand at the temple entrance, armed with wooden clubs. Meanwhile

E*

another crowd of men had gathered opposite them, also armed with clubs. These were men who had to discharge a vow they had made to the god. The few priests attending Set now put him, in his shrine, into a four-wheeled cart which they dragged along to the temple. The other priests, at the temple entrance, tried to prevent it from entering, while the crowd of men under a vow to the god attacked them with their clubs. Herodotus was of the opinion that in the ensuing struggle many heads were broken and several men were actually killed, or died of the injuries they received, though the local Egyptians told him that fatalities were unknown.

There was a legend to explain the origin of this custom. Set's mother, so it was said, lived once in the temple, but Set was brought up elsewhere. On attaining manhood he went in search of his mother, but her attendants, not knowing who he was, prevented him from entering the temple; so he went off to another town, raised a body of companions and, returning with them, fought his way in.

The legend of Osiris and Set is in many ways thought-provoking. Osiris was a just and benevolent king of Egypt; his brother Set, out of jealousy, planned to murder him. He first made ready a magnificent chest, then invited his brother and some of his own friends and fellow-conspirators to a feast. He told the guests he would give the chest to anyone who, lying inside it, found it fitted him. One by one the guests got into the chest, and found it did not fit them. When Osiris's turn came, as soon as he lay down inside it Set slammed the lid shut and fastened it down, and the chest was thrown into the Nile.

Osiris's wife Isis succeeded in recovering the body, but Set stole it back and cut it into fourteen pieces, which were scattered throughout Egypt. Isis found them all, with the aid of her sister Nephthys, and reunited them by magic. By magic also she succeeded in conceiving a child, who was Horus. Horus was brought up in secret, despite attempts by Set to capture him, such as that he made at Buto which the children's guardian thwarted by concealing them in the floating island of Chemmis. So Horus grew up, and sought vengeance on Set, against whom he prevailed in the end.

The story is perhaps the earliest known example of the death-and-resurrection legend which exerts a continuous fascination for the human mind, with its encouragement of the bizarre but deep-rooted desire of the human ego for permanence.

Busiris, the next city on Herodotus's itinerary, stood in the geographical middle of Lower Egypt, on the west bank of the Phatnitic or Bucolic branch of the Nile. This was one of the seven major branches of the river at that time, but it was an artificial one, a channel that had been cut to connect with the Sebennytic branch. The major feature of the city was an immense temple to Isis. Busiris was much venerated as a place of pilgrimage, and its festival of Isis was second only in importance to that of Bast at Bubastis. Isis was the great mother, wife of Osiris and mother of Horus and Bast, the equivalent of the Greek Demeter. She introduced the cultivation of wheat and barley, and sheaves of these were carried at her festival. This was attended, Herodotus says, by tens of thousands of men and women who, when the sacrifices were over, beat their breasts: but in whose honour he prefers not to say.

This peculiar hesitation of Herodotus in speaking—or not speaking —of Osiris stems probably from the resemblance of the "passion play" of Osiris to some of the mysteries of Dionysus. This was so close that Herodotus felt it was trespassing dangerously on ground sacred to him to go into any detail of the mystical attributes of Osiris, though he is happy enough to mention him in less delicate matters.

The beating of the breast in mourning for the death of Osiris was a proper part of the sacrifices to Isis, but Osiris's own cult centre was at Abydos in Upper Egypt, which Herodotus certainly passed and probably visited on his journey to Elephantine.

Herodotus believed that much of the Greek religion of his time originated in Egypt. The names of all the Greek gods, for instance, came from there; they certainly came from abroad, and it was most likely that it was Egypt they came from, since the names of all the gods had been known there since the beginning of time. Only a few, such as Poseidon, were not of Egyptian origin; the Pelasgians, predecessors of the Greeks, learned of him from the Libyans, who had always known his name and always worshipped him. Herodotus is of the opinion that Homer and Hesiod—a Boeotian who lived about a hundred years later than Homer—were the first to describe the gods, giving them their correct titles, functions and attributes.

The idea of the importation of gods from Egypt is a charming one and of course reasonable enough, since Herodotus was firmly of the opinion that the gods existed, so that the knowledge of their names and natures might well be passed on by gradual revelation from nation to nation. The universal tendency of mankind to invent and partake in religious beliefs and practices is more clearly recognized in modern times, but the majority of people—even of psychologists and anthropologists—are still debarred as effectively as Herodotus, if they are believers in a particular religion or unconsciously committed to the cultural tradition in which they were brought up, from a perception any clearer than his of the nature of gods.

After Herodotus's time the worship of Isis really did spread to

Greece and became widely practised there. In later centuries it also became popular in Rome, from the time of the dictator Sulla. In 43 B.C. the triumvirs went so far as to build a temple of Isis and Serapis, to improve their standing with the people. Augustus tried to ban her worship and failed; it continued to be practised until it gradually faded away in Christian times.

From Busiris it was a cross-country journey to Bubastis, on the east bank of the Pelusian branch of the Nile, one of the principal waterways of Egypt. The river flowed past the city in a broad and majestic stream; the great boats carrying goods between the cities of Upper Egypt and the sea sixty miles away sailed past it, or pulled into its quays. Herodotus, an enthusiastic amateur of shipping and marine matters generally, took a great interest in these craft. They were made of the wood of a kind of thorn-tree that exuded gum. Short planks about three feet long were cut from this tree, laid together like bricks, and attached by long spikes to cross-tiers until the hull was completely built up, when deck planks running from side to side were laid on top. The boats had no ribs, and the seams were caulked on the inside with papyrus. There was a single steering-oar driven down through the keel; the masts were of the same wood as the hull, the sails of papyrus.

The boats could not make way upstream unless there was a brisk stern wind, so they were towed from the banks. For travelling downstream, each vessel was equipped with a raft of tamarisk bound together with reeds, and a stone weighing about four hundredweight with a hole through the middle of it. The raft was attached to the bow of the vessel by a cable, and the stone to the stern. The raft was carried down-river by the current and kept the bow pointing downstream, while the stone, dragged along the bottom, acted as a check on the motion and kept the stern upstream. There was a great number of these boats on the Nile, some of them having a capacity of many thousand talents: which comes to many hundred tons, since there are about thirty talents to the ton, the talent varying somewhat according to the locality.

Bubastis suffered somewhat under the Persian dynasty and gradually lost much of its importance, but at the time of Herodotus's visit there were few signs of this decline, and it was still a huge and bustling ity, a major centre of both commerce and religion. Sheshonq, the first pharaoh of the Twenty-second Dynasty, came from Hermopolis to establish his capital there, about 935 B.C.; much earlier still Sneferu, first king of the Fourth Dynasty in about 2600 B.C., and builder of a pyramid at Dahshur hardly smaller than that of his successor Cheops, had built at the shipyards of Bubastis a state ship of cedarwood fifty yards in length, and named it *The Adoration of the Two Lands*. He also built sixty royal barges. Trade with Byblos, north of Beirut, flourished in those distant days, cedarwood being imported from the forests of Lebanon to make up for the lack of timber in Egypt. Modern excavations have turned up there pillars inscribed with the ceremonial names of Cheops. Trade with all the eastern Mediterranean ports and those of the Red Sea, reached through Necho's enlarged canal, still flowed busily in Herodotus's time.

Bubastis was the city of Bast, the cat-goddess, sister of Horus and daughter of Isis and Osiris. All Egyptian cats were taken to Bubastis to be mummified and buried in the great cat-cemeteries there. Mummification of animals, cats included, was a trifle perfunctory, but although the body was often little more than a pickled skeleton before it was bandaged, the bandaging was carried out with great skill so that the appearance was convincing.

Bubastis, like all Egyptian cities, was of necessity raised well above the general level of the delta, to keep it clear of the floods. Herodotus relates how the pharaoh Shabaka of the Twenty-fifth, Nubian, Dynasty, instead of punishing convicted criminals by death, made them work to raise the level of the soil of their native town. The level of the ground of the cities had already been raised in the reign of Ramesses II, when many canals were dug. Herodotus thought Bubastis stood higher than any other Egyptian city. The temple of Bast was not perhaps as large as that of some other cities, and may not have cost as much to build, but none, he considered, gave more pleasure to the eye. It was built on what was almost an island, since two canals had been led from the Nile round each side of the temple enclosure until they reached the entrance, where they stopped short without meeting. The canals were each a hundred feet wide and shaded with trees. The temple gateway was sixty feet high and was decorated with carved figures nine feet high.

The temple was in the middle of the city, and since the level of the buildings everywhere else had been raised, but that of the temple had not, it was possible to look down on it and get an excellent view of it from across the canal on all sides. It was surrounded by a low wall with figures carved on it, and within the enclosure there was a grove of tall trees surrounding the shrine, which was very large and contained a statue of Bast. The enclosure was square in plan, each side a furlong in length. The temple was approached by a stone-paved road four hundred feet wide, running through the market-place, and joining the temple of Bast at one end with a temple of the ibis-headed god Thoth (whom Herodotus associates with Hermes the herald and messenger of the gods) at the other. The road was lined on both sides with trees, so tall that they seemed to touch the sky.

The annual festival of the cat-goddess at Bubastis was the most important of all the festivals of Egypt, and was attended by the greatest numbers of people, as many as seven hundred thousand men and women—not counting the children—assembling there. They came in barges down the river and the canals, each boat containing a great throng of men and women together, some of them playing musical instruments—the men playing flutes and the women castanets—while the rest sang and clapped their hands to the rhythm of the music. When they passed a town on the banks they would bring the boat close inshore, and the women would exchange shouts and abuse with the women of the town, dancing or hitching up their skirts in an insulting fashion. The festival itself was celebrated with lavish sacrifices, and an immense amount of wine was consumed in Bubastis, more than during the whole of the rest of the year.

Herodotus obviously had warm memories of Bubastis, with its beautiful temple, its wide tree-shaded streets and its lively river-life. Little remains of it now but the mound of Tell-Basta, the Hill of Bast, on the outskirts of Zagazig.

He seems to have passed by Athribis, or ignored it, and made for Heliopolis, the city of the sun-god Re or Ra, whose people, he thought, were the most learned in Egypt. He talked to them a great deal about religion, but he does not care to repeat what he learned, apart from the names of their deities, since in his opinion no nation knows much more about such things than any other, so that there is no point in comparing their views. As for more practical matters, the Egyptians told him—and he believed them—that they were the first to discover the solar year and divide it into twelve parts. In his opinion their method of doing so was better than that of the Greeks, since they divided it into twelve months each of thirty days, leaving five days over as additional ones, whereas the Greeks put in an extra month every other year to make the seasons work out properly. And he reiterates that they were also the first to bring into use the names of the gods, which the Greeks learned from them, and to construct altars, images and temples for their worship, and carve figures in stone. They told him how they had been the first to do all these things, and he agreed, being an exceptionally agreeable character.

They also told him that the first ruler of Egypt was Min; that is, Menes, or Narmer, the first king of the first dynasty, who unified the north and south in about 3100 B.C., by which time writing was in use, records could be kept and more complex administrations than those of pre-dynastic times became possible. In the days of Min, the priests of Heliopolis told him, the whole country, except the district around Thebes, was marsh, and none of the land below Lake Moeris—seven days' voyage up-river from the sea—showed above water. In this they were not wholly correct, since the delta is somewhat older than that; on the other hand it is true that in the time of Menes/Narmer a great deal of it must have consisted of marshland and scrub.

As for Heliopolis as a centre of religion, fortunately Herodotus, who is so reluctant to disclose what the priests of Heliopolis told him, is not the only source of information available to us. The original sun-god of Heliopolis was called Tum or Atum: later Re took over his attributes from him. The universe, according to the doctrines accepted at Heliopolis, was in the beginning a watery chaos called Nun, from which the sun-god Atum emerged. By a kind of parthenogenesis Atum gave birth to Shu, the god of air, and Tefmut, the goddess of moisture. They, mating, produced the earth-god, Geb, and the sky-goddess, Nut: and these two produced Osiris, Isis, Set and Nephthys, another guardian of the viscera-jars. These nine gods were the ennead, the company of gods sometimes regarded as a triple equivalent of the trinity, a nine-in-one. A conventional picture of the world showed Shu, standing, supporting the naked body of Nut, which, curving, formed the arch of heaven, while Geb lay at his feet.

There were other cosmogonies at Hermopolis and Memphis, but all these were somehow blended as time went on into one acceptable system; one of the many agreeable and civilized attributes of the Egyptians being the ability to believe several different things at once, in contrast with the puritan barbarism that regards one tiny aspect of truth, seen (as human beings see it) through a narrow slit in a fog with defective vision, as excluding all others.

The religion of Egypt, as viewed from Heliopolis, was a sophisticated and subtle conception; the dancers in the streets of Sais or Bubastis regarded it in a simpler light. Most religions know a similar gradation in their adherents. Heliopolis was indeed a learned place, as Herodotus saw it to be, a place of high theology, along with Hermopolis and Memphis. In their temples the Jesuits of the Heliopolitan ennead and the Hermopolitan ogdoad (they had eight gods instead of nine) learned their hierographical paces.

If different theological systems and a profusion of greater and lesser gods co-existed, ritual tended to become standardized. The manner of worship of Re at Heliopolis gradually spread and became the norm in the temples of all the gods. This was so in part because of the devotion to Re that became widespread during the Fifth Dynasty. From that time on, all kings of Egypt were regarded as sons of Re, so that the ritual of worship of any god, in which the king symbolized the central participant, involved the identification to some extent of the local god or goddess with Re. As the worship of Osiris spread during the Middle Kingdom period (2080–1786), the two systems involving the father-son relationship of Re and the king, on the one hand, and Osiris and Horus, on the other, merged and blended in a characteristic Egyptian compromise: it was a religion with ecumenism built in.

There were the usual annual assemblies, which at Heliopolis were devoted to the sun-god, but it is clear from the paucity of his information about the assembly at Heliopolis that Herodotus was not there at the appropriate time to see it.

The veneration of mummified bulls was a practice at Heliopolis as it was at Memphis. A creature more intimately associated with the sun-city was the phoenix. Herodotus says that he saw this sacred bird only in paintings, which depicted it as similar to an eagle in shape and size, with red and gold plumage. They told him at Heliopolis that it lived in Arabia and visited Egypt only once every five hundred years, when the parent bird died. When this happened the succeeding phoenix, its son, looked for a lump of myrrh as big as it could carry, hollowed it out, put the body of its parent inside it and sealed it in by smearing some more myrrh over the hole. It then picked it up and flew with it to the temple of the sun at Heliopolis, where it buried it. It then returned to Arabia and there built itself a nest, to which it imparted the magical power of giving birth to the next phoenix. When, after five hundred years, it died, a new phoenix arose from the nest, to wrap its parent up in myrrh and carry him to Heliopolis.

Such was the life-cycle of the phoenix, as recounted to Herodotus. There are other versions of the legend, of which the most familiar is that in which at the age of five hundred the phoenix, feeling his end approaching, builds for himself a funeral pyre of spices, settles upon it, sings a melodious dirge and, flapping its wings to make a better draught, is consumed by flames. After its death a new phoenix arises from the ashes. This version, however, since it involved no journey to Heliopolis, was not likely to be popular there.

The reign of the Ptolemies, that began a hundred and fifty years after Herodotus's visit, was fatal to Heliopolis. It decayed gradually owing to the disorders in the country during the last two centuries of their rule. In 30 B.C. Mark Antony was defeated at Actium, Cleopatra committed suicide and the Romans moved in. Strabo, visiting the site of Heliopolis in the early years of the Roman occupation, found it totally deserted.

Southwards of Heliopolis Herodotus came to the narrows where the Nile is hemmed in on the east by the Arabian mountains running

Herodotus's Westward Journey to Italy and Greece

Mounted warrior from Italy (Lucania) c. 500 B.C.

The Athenian parthenon to the left, and Cimon's tomb on the right. Athens became the point of departure and intellectual repository for Herodotus' life work: his quest for civilization.

north and south, and on the west by the range of rocky and sandy hills where the pyramids stand. In the mountains to the east were the quarries where the stone was cut for the pyramids of Memphis.

The city of Memphis was, so the priests told him, built by Menes, who also diverted the river from the site of the city, through which it used to flow, and built a dam to protect the city from the floods. The Persian authorities at the time of his visit had to keep a careful watch on the dam, since if it burst the city would be overwhelmed. Menes was also said to have built the temple of Ptah.

Herodotus identified Ptah with Hephaestus, the Greek god of fire, son of Zeus and Hera, the Vulcan of the Romans. He was born lame, so that in distaste his mother hurled him down from Olympus, but this did him no harm, except to give him the sort of bumptiousness associated with deep-seated feelings of insecurity. He became the patron god of cuckolded husbands, owing to the carryings on of his wife Aphrodite with the ridiculous Ares, but apart from this he was an artist, particularly skilled in working in metals, and it is in his artist-capacity that Herodotus sees him as equivalent to Ptah, since Ptah was the great creator-god and the patron god of craftsmen. The equivalence is very weak, since Ptah was a cut or two above Hephaestus, and besides that was by no means a son of Amun/Zeus, or even a relation of his, being an original god of Memphis while Amun was an original god of Thebes.

The temple of Ptah was large and splendid. In front of it there was a recumbent statue seventy-five feet long, presented by Amasis, like the similar one at Heliopolis. Amasis also built a temple of Isis at Memphis that Herodotus describes as "spacious and remarkable". South of the temple of Ptah there was a district occupied by Phoenicians from Tyre, and in it was a temple of Aphrodite the Stranger. There were many other temples, Memphis being the centre of many cults.

A particular object of reverence at Memphis was the bull-god, Apis. The Egyptians believed that Apis took the form of the offspring of a young cow on whom a ray of light had fallen from heaven, causing her to receive the god. The calf when born was recognized by certain signs to be the god. It had to be black all over except for a white square mark on the forehead, and must have a mark like an eagle on its back, double hairs in its tail and a lump or knot on its tongue resembling a scarab. When these signs were found the animal was consecrated with great ceremony and brought to Memphis, where he lived in luxurious quarters with extensive grounds for his recreation and entertainment. His birthday was celebrated every year with rejoicing, not only in Memphis but throughout Egypt. He was allowed to live only a certain number of years, and if he did not die before that time he was killed and buried in a sacred well whose site was known only to initiates. If, however, he died a natural death he was buried publicly with due solemnity, and his death was celebrated with universal mourning.

After Cambyses had conquered Egypt, and while he was staying at Memphis, the god Apis was found to have manifested himself and was brought to Memphis. This caused great joy among the people, who at once ceased work, put on their best clothes and started celebrating. Cambyses, seeing this, assumed that they were rejoicing over the recent disaster that had overtaken him when he had set off to conquer Ethiopia and lost a large part of his army in the desert. He summoned some of the leading citizens and asked them why they had not celebrated when he first arrived in the city but had waited until he returned there after his defeat? They told him that a god had just appeared among them, that this happened only at long intervals of time, and that whenever it did so they rejoiced and celebrated a festival. Cambyses told his informants they were lying, and had them executed. Summoning the priests of Memphis, he asked them the same question and received the same answer. He ordered them to show him the god, and they brought him the bull-calf Apis. On this, he drew his dagger and struck at the calf's belly, but missed his aim and wounded it in the thigh: a similar wound to that which he later inflicted on himself at Ecbatana in Syria, and of which he died. He had the priests whipped, and commanded that the festival should be terminated forthwith. The people were to return to their ordinary occupations, and anyone who continued to take a holiday would be put to death. So the festival ended abruptly, and the god Apis was led away to the temple, where the wound in his thigh festered, until he died and was secretly buried by the priests.

Cambyses brought ruin and woe to Memphis, laying waste several sections of the city. It was no doubt this circumstance that led Herodotus to indulge in little description of this still magnificent city. It was still splendid long after his time, but at the time he saw it the wounds were recent.

He did, however, visit the pyramids, as any tourist should, and describes in detail the three pyramids of Giza—those of Cheops, Chephren and Mycerinus—and the labour of building them. He was greatly impressed by the roadway along which the blocks to build the pyramid of Cheops were hauled; according to his account, it took a labour force of a hundred thousand men, working in three-monthly stints, ten years to build this roadway, which was five furlongs in length, sixty feet wide and forty-eight feet high at its highest point, and constructed of polished stone blocks decorated with carvings of animals. At the same time the underground burial chambers on the site on which the pyramid was to be built were excavated. The building of the pyramid itself took twenty years. Its base was square, each side measuring eight hundred feet, and its height was equal to the length of one side; none of the blocks of which it was built was less than thirty feet long.

It was built up in tiers. When the base layer was completed the blocks were lifted to the next level by a device which Herodotus describes only in so far as to say that it was made up from short timbers. On completion of the first tier a similar device at that level lifted the blocks for the next. When the basic structure of the pyramid was completed the finishing off of the outer surface was carried out from the top downwards.

In recent times there has been a tendency among Egyptologists to contend that the idea of vast armies of permanent slave labour is a misreading of the situation, and that the labourers were recruited from the ordinary peasantry during the slack seasons of the Egyptian farming year. It may indeed be true that the majority of the pyramid-labourers were not in the strict sense of the word slaves, but this is not to say that even the smallest fraction of them came willingly, or failed to experience intense fatigue, pain and hunger during much or all of their compulsory labour. Herodotus had the advantages as well as the disadvantages of a man who hears the history of a country from its common people rather than from its experts or its historians, who tend to peer over the tops of the common herd and dismiss anything they have to say as inconsiderable. Much is seen from above that is not perceptible from below, but the reverse also holds. If the memory of Cheops was loathed among the ordinary people of Egypt more than two thousand years later, as Herodotus found that it was, it may be that the ordinary people still felt the bruises of their forefathers which the more fortunate had been aided by their own present comforts to forget.

The resultant work has been described as one of the most impressive edifices ever constructed by man, but the cost of constructing it was far beyond anything that the revenue of the country could justify and represented ruin for the economy of Egypt besides an immeasurable amount of avoidable suffering for its people.

After Cheops, his successor Chephren built a pyramid about forty feet lower, and the general exhaustion and grief of Egypt continued. Chephren also observed an interesting mass of natural rock and had it hewn out into the Sphinx, which bears what is probably a representation of his face. It is one of the strange omissions of Herodotus's book that he makes no mention of it, though there can be no doubt that he saw it.

Mycerinus, the successor of Cheops and Chephren, was in many ways a notable improvement on his exceptionally unappealing predecessors, but even he felt compelled to build a pyramid of his own, though it is much smaller than that of Cheops, its sides being a mere two hundred and eighty feet long.

Westwards of the Nile, thirty miles south of Memphis, and lying rather less than ten miles from the river at its nearest point, is the natural depression called El-Faiyûm. It stretches about forty-five miles from east to west, and about twenty-eight miles from north to south, the entire area—depression and surrounding fertile land— being roughly a triangle with its base downwards. It has an area now of 850 square miles. There is a break in the hills on the west bank of the Nile through which the road to the town of El-Faiyûm now leads. This provided access long ago for the canal which led the flood waters of the Nile through to form, in the northern part of the depression, the lake now called Birket Qârûn, and in Herodotus's time Lake Moeris. With its surrounding marshes it was always from the most ancient times a splendid place for wildfowling and hunting.

The area was particularly important to the kings of the Twelfth Dynasty. Sesostris I established his capital near the entrance to it, at Itj-Towy. The greatest monarch of the dynasty was Ammenemes III, whose personal name was Nymare or Ni-Maat-Re (which means "Re is in possession of the Truth") and was known to Herodotus by the name of Moeris, a corruption of Nymare. He was young at his accession—possibly not much more than twenty—and reigned 46 years.

It was Ammenemes III who had floodgates built at each end of the canal leading from the Nile to Lake Moeris, so that the waters could be controlled. In Herodotus's time water flowed from the Nile into Lake Moeris for six months of the year and out again for six months, so that Lake Moeris acted as a reservoir both to control the flood-waters and give them back to the irrigation systems when they were most needed.

It was Moeris who built the labyrinth, possibly the most extra-ordinary monument of all. Herodotus said it was beyond his power to describe it. The pyramids were astonishing structures, but the labyrinth surpassed them all. As he describes it, it had twelve covered courts, six in a row facing north, six facing south, the gates of those in one row exactly opposite the gates of the other, with a continuous wall round the outside of the whole. The building contained altogether three thousand rooms, half of them being underground and the other half directly above these.

His guides took him through the rooms in the upper storey, but would not show him the underground rooms, since they contained the tombs of the kings who had built them, besides the tombs of the sacred crocodiles. The upper rooms, which he did see, were enough to baffle the imagination, and it was hard to believe that they were made by men. The passages communicating from court to court and from room to room were an endless wonder to him, as he passed with his guides from courtyard to room, from room to gallery, from gallery to more rooms, from rooms into yet more galleries and thence into yet more courtyards. The roofs of every courtyard, room and gallery were of stone, as were the walls. The walls were covered with carved figures, and every court was walled with white marble and surrounded by a colonnade. At one corner of the labyrinth there was a pyramid forty feet high with carved figures of animals on it, and an underground passage by which it could be entered.

The labyrinth was, as other visitors, Greek and Roman, have made clear, a collection of palaces with, behind them, as many chapels as there were nomes—administrative districts—of Egypt. According to Strabo, a deputation from any nome visiting the labyrinth went to the chapel representing their own nome, and there performed their sacrifices and discussed and passed judgment on questions of major importance concerning it. On the walls of each chapel was inscribed all the essential information about that particular nome: the delimitation of its frontiers, the taxes it had to pay, its legal rights in the vital matter of water supply, and details of its cults, temples and monuments. It was a filing system in stone, a complete directory of the nome, where the deputation, come to meet in committee, could check the exact statement of their rights and their obligations towards the state, that is, the king.

It was the immensity of the monument that amazed these visitors above all else. The roof of the labyrinth formed one single solid surface of stone slabs, so vast that they felt, standing on it, that they were in the middle of an immense plain of stone. The complex of rooms below was so extensive and so intricate, and joined by such a maze of galleries that, as Herodotus says, strangers could only find their way about with the aid of a guide. The word "labyrinth" itself, which reaches us through the Greek "labyrinthos", is almost certainly derived from the Egyptian word for the original labyrinth, though exactly what that word was is unknown.

The labyrinth at once calls to mind a monument of much more recent times, the Great Hall of the People in Peking. Here, too, is one room for each province of China, where delegations from that province meet and refresh themselves—with tea rather than religious observances—before proceeding to discuss matters of interest concerning the province; though the stone roof resembling an immense plain is missing here, as the auditorium and offices of the National People's Congress were from the labyrinth by Lake Moeris.

Herodotus thought Lake Moeris itself hardly less astonishing than the labyrinth. It was obviously man-made, since nearly in the middle of it, standing three hundred feet out of the water, were two pyramids, whose bases were said to be an equal depth below the surface. At the summit of each pyramid was a stone statue of a man seated on a throne. The water of the lake was not supplied by natural springs, of which there were none in the country thereabouts, but had been brought from the Nile through an artificial channel. So says Herodotus, adding the interesting detail that during the six months of the year that the water was running out of the lake the local authorities had to pay to the king's treasury a talent—sixty to eighty pounds—of silver for the fish that were caught, but during the six months when it was running back again only a third of that amount.

Of the city of Crocodilopolis, whose ruins now stand on the outskirts of the town of El-Faiyûm, Herodotus says little; he was more interested in the labyrinth, Lake Moeris, and, of course, the crocodiles themselves. He describes the crocodile as a four-footed, amphibious creature which took no food during the winter months. It spent most of the day on land, where it laid and hatched its eggs, and the whole of the night in the river, where the water was warmer than the night air. The difference in size between the infant crocodile and the full-grown one was greater than that for any other living creature, since a crocodile's egg was hardly any bigger than that of a goose, and the young when hatched were much the same size as newly-hatched geese, but the adult grew to a length of twenty-three feet or more. A greater growth from infancy is shown by another large animal of which Herodotus however knew nothing, the kangaroo.

The crocodile had little eyes like a pig's, but its teeth were huge fangs out of proportion to the size of its head; it was the only animal to have no tongue, and a fixed lower jaw. This did not move, so that when eating the crocodile brought the upper jaw down on the lower. It had powerful jaws and a scaly hide, so tough that its back was impenetrable by any weapon. It could not see at all under water, though it had excellent sight on land.

As a result of spending so much time in the water the inside of its mouth was covered with leeches. All other animals avoided the crocodile with one exception, the sandpiper or Egyptian plover. This was of great service to the crocodile, since when the latter came ashore and lay on the ground with its mouth wide open (Herodotus says it usually faced west) the bird hopped in and ate the leeches. In consequence the crocodile, recognizing this as a contribution to its comfort, never harmed the bird, and the two lived together in the greatest amity.

In all this, Herodotus's observation is at its most acute, and it is obvious that he must have spent considerable time on the Nile and round about Lake Moeris watching crocodiles and noting their ways.

Some Egyptians, he says, looked on the crocodile as a sacred beast, while others did not, but treated it as an enemy. Those who revered it most were those who lived near Lake Moeris and at Thebes. Here the custom was to keep a crocodile in luxurious captivity, inserting rings in its ears and bracelets on its forefeet, feeding it on food of the highest quality and making offerings to it. When it died they embalmed it and buried it in a consecrated sepulchre. On the other hand, in the neighbourhood of Elephantine crocodiles were not considered sacred at all, but were hunted, killed and eaten.

The crocodile was in fact revered through most of Egypt, as was the crocodile-god Sobk. Local ways were very strong, however, and a natural tendency to kill crocodiles had not yet given way everywhere in Upper Egypt to the softening effects of religion. Herodotus gives details of a method of catching them which he regards as the most ingenious among many others. A hook was baited with a lump of pork and allowed to float on its line out to midstream. At the same time the hunter, standing on the bank, beat a live pig, so that it emitted loud squeals. The crocodile came hurtling through the water towards the pig, encountered the bait on the way and swallowed it along with the hook; it was then pulled out of the water. When it was hauled on to the bank the first thing the hunter did was to plaster its eyes all over with mud. It was then possible to kill it without much difficulty, but without this precaution it was liable to give a good deal of trouble.

El-Faiyûm fascinated Herodotus, as well it might. Egypt is altogether singular; it is like nowhere else in the world. El-Faiyûm is like nowhere else in Egypt.

There are times in any journey when the aim of the journey takes over from the interest of the journey itself: the arriving seems more important than the travelling. This seems to have happened to Herodotus after he left El-Faiyûm: he had one overriding desire, to get to Elephantine. He had taken in countless new impressions in the delta and in Lake Moeris, and, admirable traveller though he was, for a time he took in few more. As he travelled up the river he passed the extraordinary monuments of Upper Egypt: he must have looked at them, or some of them, but apart from a few stray comments he has nothing to say about them. The Ultima Thule of his journey, Elephantine, called him on, and he had few eyes for anything along the way.

It was, he reckoned, nine days' journey from Heliopolis to Thebes, or 550 miles. (It is always a bad sign when a traveller begins to reckon up how long his journey is; he had done the same thing travelling from the Kerch Strait to Colchis.) Given the twists and turns in the Nile, this is about right, though without them it is about a hundred miles shorter. Not far from the entrance to El-Faiyûm he passed by Heracleopolis Magna, the place from which Sheshonq I the Libyan set out to found the Twenty-Second Dynasty. There the ram-headed god Arsaphis was once the supreme object of worship. Then there was Cynopolis, the home of the jackal-god Anubis, and after it Oxyrhynchus, where the sharp-snouted fish of the same name was sacred to the cow-goddess Hathor.

Further south, on the west bank, was Hermopolis, the burial-place of the sacred ibis and cult-centre of the ibis-headed god Thoth, inventor of writing and scribe of the gods, to whom the ape was also sacred; this was one of the most ancient cities of Egypt. On the east, no great distance further on, was Akhetaten, built in a hurry of unburnt bricks by the eccentric Akhenaten, the mystic visionary who married the beautiful Nefertiti (though one or two representations of her show a dumpy woman with a rustic face); rejected all the gods in favour of the one true god, Aten, the sun-disc with the glorious rays, and was succeeded (after the brief reign of one Smenkhkare) by the well-known Tutankhamun, who restored all the gods that Akhenaten had deposed. The site of Akhenaten's dream-palace from which he ruled his dream-kingdom is now known as Tell el-Amârna.

Next, far away to the south, where the Nile emerges from its great eastern bend, was Abydos—another and a very different Abydos from the one on the Hellespont that Herodotus had visited a few years before. This was the principal cult-centre of Osiris, a city second only in power and fame in Upper Egypt to Thebes itself, with a temple where there were to be seen many tombs of ancient kings of the earlier dynasties; the temple was begun by Sethos I of the Nineteenth Dynasty and completed by Ramesses II, who succeeded him. It is just possible that Herodotus may have stopped off for a time here, interrupting his voyage south, since he describes the festival of Dionysus/Osiris, which was certainly held at Abydos; but in view of his failure even to mention the name of the place it is rather more likely that he saw the Dionysus-procession somewhere else. It involved small puppets with enormous genitals operated by strings, which were made to move up and down as the women carried them round the villages, preceded by flutes, and singing a hymn to the orgiastic god.

Then there was Tentyra, where there were temples of Hathor, Isis and Set, and where the people were noted for their intense hatred of crocodiles; and, opposite it, Chemmis, which Herodotus certainly called in at, however briefly, since the people there told him that it was the ancestral home of the Greek god Perseus. Perseus's fore-fathers, Danaus and Lynceus, were Chemmites who emigrated from there to Greece, so they told him. Perseus was frequently to be seen in the neighbourhood, occasionally leaving behind him a sandal three feet long. After slaying the Gorgon he brought her head to Chemmis, having heard of the place from his mother Danaë, and visited his relations there. There was a square of enclosed ground at Chemmis sacred to Perseus, Herodotus says, with palm trees surrounding it, and a very large stone gateway with two equally large stone figures on top of it. Within the temple enclosure there was a shrine with a statue of Perseus, and in his worship athletic contests on the Greek model were held, with prizes of cattle, cloaks and hides. Chemmis was later known as Panopolis, and a thousand years after Herodotus's visit the Greek Christian poet Nonnus was born there.

He went on past Ombos, where the worship of the crocodile was fervent, and Coptos, almost opposite it, where a road from the Red Sea reached the Nile, and the worship of the ithyphallic Min flourished in predynastic times. Then, coming near the other end of the bend in the Nile, he was at Thebes.

Thebes was the chief city of Upper Egypt, for long ages the capital city of the whole country, and was reputed—along with a few other cities, but not very many—to be the oldest city in the world. It was the chief seat of the worship of Amun, and Homer said of it that it had a hundred gates, from each of which it could send out two hundred war-chariots fully armed. He exaggerated; but if ever there were great cities, Thebes was one of them. It had reached the pinnacle of its splendour a thousand years earlier, but it was still great among the greatest cities. Surrounding it were Karnak, Luxor and the Valley of the Kings, abounding in a profusion of temples, colossi, sphinxes, obelisks and royal tombs of the utmost magnificence.

Yet all Herodotus says of Thebes is that crocodiles were sacred there; that the Thebans never sacrificed sheep but only goats (this was because the ram was sacred to Amun); and that rain never fell there. And all that he says of the surrounding country is that near Thebes there was to be found a species of snake sacred to Zeus. They were small and quite harmless and had two horns growing from the tops of their heads, and if any of them were found dead they were buried in the temple of Amun.

Such was the magic of Thebes, as Herodotus saw it. But some travellers among us cannot respond to an expected magic; and this disability affects more travellers, perhaps, than are ready to confess it. Those who have lived for several weeks in Athens without visiting the Acropolis, or who have found the Grand Canyon rather disappointing, may salute him wryly over a vast space of years as a fellow-spirit. It is strange that so often over the centuries he has been accused of being dishonest, when his honesty is so transparent it is sometimes almost embarrassing. He has nothing to say about Thebes, so he says nothing, where a lesser man would have pretended to be excited by something that—perhaps out of travel-fatigue, or a disorder in his digestion—left him flat. The one thing that aroused a flicker of his temporarily flagging interest was the horned snakes, and heaven knows what they can have been; there have been many speculations, all fruitless. There is no explaining them, and the one certain thing is that Herodotus was not lying, since if he had wanted to lie he surely would have found something more important to lie about than these absurd snakes.

The travel-fury drove him onward from Thebes, up the long, narrow, slowly winding valley of the Nile. Elephantine, his goal, he estimated at 210 miles ahead. They passed Hermonthis, where the falcon-headed Month, or Munt, was worshipped, and bulls were sacred. Then there was Hieraconpolis, once a capital of Upper Egypt, cult-centre of Horus. At Edfu the limestone cliffs that had walled in the valley since Heliopolis gave way to red sandstone; there was a temple of Horus here. Once again, Herodotus is silent on all these things; there are not even any rumours of suicidal cats or horned snakes in the country between Thebes and Elephantine.

The ruins of Elephantine are just outside the modern Aswan. It was the limit of Herodotus's southward journey for the excellent reason that it was the limit of the Persian Empire. There was a Persian frontier post there, and Herodotus had no intention of going past it into the country beyond.

As he himself says: "As far as Elephantine I speak as an eye-witness, but further south from hearsay." What lay on the south was the First Cataract of the Nile. What he learned from hearsay was that beyond Elephantine the country rose steeply, so that in that part of the river boats had to be hauled along by ropes, one on each side, as an ox is dragged. If the ropes parted the boat was at once carried away by the force of the stream.

This steep ascent went on for four days' journey, the river winding sharply all the time, and above it there was another level plain, where the river was divided by an island called Tachompso. Beyond this was a great lake, round whose shores lived tribes of nomadic Ethiopians. On the far side of the lake was the place where the Nile flowed into it. Here it was necessary to land, leave the boats, and travel along the bank of the river for forty days, since sharp rocks, some showing above the water and some submerged, made it impossible to travel by boat. Here he is speaking of the second and third cataracts. After the forty days' journey on land along the banks of the river the traveller embarked in another boat and journeyed up-river for twelve more days to Meroë, said to be the capital city of the Ethiopians.

This is a by no means fanciful description of the journey up the Nile to the ancient city of Merowe, 120 miles north-east of Khartoum. Merowe was a capital of the kingdom of Ethiopia from about 700–300 B.C., and was its capital therefore in the days of Herodotus. Excavations there in the earlier parts of this century revealed the ruins of palaces and temples, with groups of pyramids nearby.

Beyond Merowe his account becomes vaguer and more fanciful, but, as he says, all this was hearsay. His account of the Ethiopians themselves is not without interest. They were said to be the tallest and best-looking people in the world. They had their own customs and their own laws, and a highly individual method of selecting their king; he was simply the man who was the tallest, and who was strong in proportion to his height. Most of the Ethiopians lived to the age of 120, some longer, and they ate boiled meat and drank milk. Cambyses had sent an embassy there to find out what they could about the Ethiopians, whom he proposed to attack. The envoys showed surprise at such longevity, whereon the Ethiopians showed them a spring whose water smelt of violets and made a man's skin glisten when he washed in it, as if he had bathed in oil. The water was of such low density that nothing would float in it, not even the lightest wood. It was their constant use of this spring that made them live to such a great age. The Ethiopians in their turn asked what the Persians ate. On being told that they ate bread, and being given an account of the way in which wheat was cultivated, they said it was not surprising that the Persians hardly ever lived beyond the age of eighty, since they lived on dung. They would probably die even younger, the Ethiopians added, if they did not drink this excellent wine, of which the envoys had brought them a sample.

The Ethiopians also showed the Persian king's envoys an object called the Table of the Sun. This was in a meadow outside the city of Meroë where the magistrates were enjoined by law to place a supply

F

of boiled meat every night, so that anybody who wished could come and eat it. It was, Herodotus says, commonly believed in the locality that the meat appeared there of its own accord and was a gift of the earth, rather than of the magistrates.

The envoys were also shown the prisons, where the prisoners were tethered with gold chains, since in Ethiopia gold was a commoner metal than bronze. Finally they were taken to see the coffins in which the Ethiopians were buried. These were made of crystal. The corpse was first dried, by a similar process to that used by the Egyptian embalmers, then covered with a layer of gypsum, which was painted to resemble the man when he was alive. It was then enclosed in a cylinder of crystal hollowed out to receive it. This material was readily available, being mined locally in large quantities, and was easily worked. The corpse was clearly visible inside the cylinder, but there was no disagreeable smell or any other inconvenient phenomenon. The relations kept the body in its crystal cylinder in their house for a year, performing sacrifices to it; then it was taken out and set upright in a special place near the town.

More reliable information regarding the Ethiopians was already known to Herodotus, since he had heard eye-witness accounts of Ethiopians who had served in Xerxes' army in its invasion of Greece. They wore leopard-skins or lion-skins and carried long bows, up to six feet long, made of the wood of the palm tree. With these they shot small cane arrows tipped with heads of stone sharpened to a fine point. They also used spears with antelope-horn heads, and knotted clubs. When going into battle they painted their bodies with chalk and vermilion. These Ethiopians also served in the army Xerxes left behind with Mardonius when he retired to Asia after the defeat at Salamis.

Such was the most substantial news Herodotus could obtain of the country beyond Elephantine. The city of Elephantine itself was built on an island in the Nile. There was a triad of gods there: Khnum, the ram-headed god of the cataract and the regions surrounding it, who was said to have moulded man on a potter's wheel; his wife Anukis, represented as a woman with a tall feather head-dress, and their daughter Satis, represented as a woman wearing a white crown with antelope-horns. There was an oratory to these three built by Ameno-phis III of the Fifteenth Dynasty, who reigned from 1417 B.C. to 1379, and many other splendid temples. But of all this Herodotus says nothing. Nor does he mention the other works of the Egyptians beyond what were her southernmost limits in his time, which he did not have the opportunity of visiting himself. There was Philae, a city on another island, just below the First Cataract; the island had extremely fertile soil, so that the vine and the fig not only flourished there but also never shed their leaves throughout the year. It had temples to Isis and other deities, and was said to be the burial-place of Isis and Osiris. Further up the Nile still, 145 miles from Elephantine, were some of the greatest monuments of all, the two temples built by Ramesses II (1304–1237 B.C.) of the Nineteenth Dynasty, in the sandstone cliffs on the left bank of the Nile, with the four immense seated figures of the king. These were the monuments later known as Abu Simbel.

When the Nile valley was flooded above Aswan by the building of the High Dam, a long, thin lake was created, stretching two hundred miles southwards into the Sudan, past Wadi Halfa. Philae was drowned in the lake; the statues at Abu Simbel were sliced into sections and reassembled at a higher level, 200 feet above their original position and twelve feet above the highest expected water level.

Sated by sightseeing, and having accomplished his purpose of reaching Elephantine, Herodotus turned back towards the north. His lack of interest in the great monuments of Upper Egypt is not, perhaps, as surprising as it may seem at first. It has to be remembered that he was, above all, a literary man, a man of words. History fascinated him; the war of his own time, the war between the Greeks and the Persians, was woven into the very stuff of his being, but he loved also to hear of the past of other peoples, their rulers and wars and movements from land to land. He was fascinated also by people, and the way of their dealings with each other, and loved above all a good story about them. He liked to hear of their customs, their food and drink and dress, their gods and their ways of worshipping them. He was interested in the way things were made and the way things worked. He had as an extra that sharp eye for topography that has already been mentioned. But, typical man of letters that he was, he had little real interest in the visual arts. In his travels in the delta this fundamental lack of interest was masked by the excitement of seeing for the first time magnificent monuments of a kind utterly strange to him, so that he will say something of temples and their dimensions and settings, even of statues, though he hardly grants them any aesthetic appeal. To paintings, though, he is sublimely indifferent. The extraordinary wealth of Egyptian art, with its exuberance, its vividness, its love of life and colour, its superb design and techniques of execution; the charm of its intimate family scenes and the sheer oddity of its depiction of men in their familiar relationship with the gods; the hunting-scenes, the charioteers, the battle-scenes full of action, the scenes of court life, the queen Nofretari playing chess in the underworld, funerals and mourners, banqueting scenes, animals, ball games, workers in various industries, archers, boats, servants at their tasks, the character revealed in portraiture the luxuriant beauty of it all, not to mention the innumerable small, enchanting objets d'art; all this, if he noticed it at all, was embraced for him by the one word: *decoration.*

It cannot be denied that this shows a regrettable one-sidedness, or at least a lack of a particular kind of sensitivity. On the other hand, no man can have all the gifts, and it might be that if he had had this one, so much prized by the modern man of culture, he might have written a duller book.

He had a few things still to see in the north, before he left Egypt for good. He travelled down to Mendes, in the north-eastern part of the delta, where the people, in contrast to those of Thebes, would not sacrifice goats but only sheep. This was because of certain resemblances between Min, the ancient god of Mendes, and goats; which Herodotus, with his usual hesitation to speak of anything remotely relating to the characteristics of Dionysus, prefers not to enlarge on.

He went on, passing perhaps through Tanis, a one-time capital of the Shepherd Kings from Arabia, and capital of the kings of the Twenty-first Dynasty, and travelled eastwards to Pelusium, near the easternmost mouth of the Nile, the Pelusian Mouth, in its muddy plain near the sea. Pelusium was the frontier city of Egypt in the east, and south of it lay the desert. There he visited the site where in 525 Cambyses broke the power of Egypt in one violent battle.

He wandered about the desert battlefield, where the bones of those who were killed still lay. There were many of them, both of Persians and of Egyptians, since the battle had been hard fought by both sides before the Egyptians were finally routed. They had been separated, the Persian dead and the Egyptian; and Herodotus noted that odd thing about the Persian warriors that he had observed before on the later battlefield at Papremis where Inarus the Libyan had routed the Persians in the beginning of his uprising. The skulls of the Persians were very thin, so thin that a light blow with a pebble would break them, but those of the Egyptians were so tough that it was hardly possible to break them with the blow of a stone. His guide, whoever he was, told him the reason was that the Egyptians shaved their heads from childhood, so that the bone of the skull was hardened by the action of the sun. It was for this reason also that the Egyptians hardly ever went bald. The Persians, on the other hand, always wore felt skull-caps, which protected their heads from the heat of the sun.

Herodotus did not leave Egypt without seeking information on a subject which, if it baffled him, is no less baffling to the modern reader, striving to understand, in this as in one or two other matters,

what in the world this gifted and indefatigably curious man is talking
about. The subject was that of flying snakes.

Someone in Egypt—it is possible that his informant may have been
a Persian—had talked to him about the natural products of Arabia,
among them such exotic spices as frankincense, myrrh, cassia,
cinnamon and the gum called ledanon. All of these except myrrh were
very troublesome to collect. The frankincense grew on trees, and the
trees on which it grew were guarded from the gatherers by great
numbers of flying snakes. The only way to drive away the flying
snakes, and so get near the trees and gather the frankincense, was to
burn below the trees the gum called storax, another kind of resin
(imported into Greece by the Phoenicians, says Herodotus) once
used in medicine.

These flying snakes were so numerous that the whole world would
swarm with them, and men would be unable to survive, if it were not
for one peculiar fact, the same fact that keeps adders from multiplying
beyond reasonable limits. This is, that with both adders and flying
snakes, at the moment of copulation the female snake seizes the male
snake by the neck and bites it through. That is the end of the male,
and the female fares little better, since when the young in her belly
achieve a certain degree of growth they gnaw at her inside until they
have eaten their way out. So the parents only get the chance to breed
once. Flying snakes do, nevertheless, seem very numerous in Arabia,
despite the self-inflicted limitation on the growth of their species, and
the reason for this is that all the flying snakes are concentrated in
Arabia, while adders, which behave in the same way, are widely
distributed all over the world and so seem less numerous.

So far, this matter of the flying snakes is not getting too far out of
hand. Frankincense, if it does not exactly grow on trees, is indeed the
resin of a tree. Someone, in some country, may have observed the
inhabitants trying to protect their productive trees of one kind or
another from being stripped of their leafage, and so destroyed, by
swarms of locusts. Putting these things together, the flying snakes
may come down merely to a third- or fourth-hand account of locust-
swarms.

Unfortunately for this theory, in the desert east of the delta, probably when he was wandering about there at the same time that he saw
the battlefield of Pelusium, he made further enquiries about the flying
snakes, since this was the nearest to Arabia he was going to get. His
informant, eager to assist in his researches, took him to a place where
he could see the skeletons of these creatures in incalculable numbers.
They were piled up in heaps, some big, some small. The place where
he saw them was a mountain pass leading to a broad plain which was

contiguous with the plain of Egypt. He was told that in the spring
the flying snakes flew towards this pass, making for Egypt, but at the
entrance to the pass they were met by armies of black ibises, which
killed them, thus preventing them from getting through to Egypt.
This valuable service was the reason why ibises were so revered in
Egypt.

The black ibis was a bird about the size of a landrail or corncrake,
jet-black all over, with legs like a crane, and a hooked beak. There
was another variety with a bald head, mostly white, but with black
throat, wing-tips and rump, but it was the black ibis that killed the
flying snakes. This is not too bad as a slightly vague description of an
ibis, but the informant also came up with a description of the winged
snake. It resembled a water-snake, and its wings were not feathered,
but more like those of a bat.

Such is the mysterious legend of the winged snake and its mortal
enemy the ibis. The piles of skeletons Herodotus saw can hardly have
been locusts, unless the locusts had been swept into heaps and were
being burned, as is the practice, and Herodotus was prevented by the
smoke from getting near enough to even one of the piles to see that
the bodies were those of insects resembling grasshoppers, rather than
of snakes.

It is still possible that he heard a story about locusts, and saw the
heaped-up skeletons of some entirely different creature; but even so,
the scene in the skeleton-haunted desert is one over which a fairly
impenetrable air of mystery broods.

He was in no hurry to return to Halicarnassus. Perhaps already he
had the feeling that when he got there he would not like it, or perhaps
it was merely that travelling had become habitual. After a certain time
in motion across the earth's surface, it begins to seem a natural way
of life; a man, or a woman, is free from all ties to place, totally
accustomed to wandering on, staying a day or two here and there and
then moving on again.

Yet home has a certain appeal. Herodotus suddenly throws in an
odd remark in Book Three: "Everyone without exception believes
his own native customs, and the religion he was brought up in, to be
the best". Possibly he did hanker for home, and if home was not
necessarily Halicarnassus, it was certainly Greece.

Still, he was in no hurry. From some port in eastern Egypt he set
off in a Greek boat going to Cyrene. Cyrene was on the first bulge of
the northern coast of Africa, five hundred miles or so west of Egypt,
about half-way between the modern cities of Tobruk and Benghazi.
It was, as has been said, a foundation of the Theran, Battus, in 631

B.C. The city was eight miles from the coast. The land rose up from the sea in two terraces, and Cyrene was on the edge of the higher, at an elevation of 1800 feet above the sea. It was supplied with water by a spring dedicated to Apollo, that rose in that spot and, having satisfied the city's needs, ran down through a delectable ravine to reach the sea at the city's harbour of Apollonia. From those heights, outside the temple of Aphrodite, the statue of the goddess presented to the city by Ladice, the wife of Amasis, looked outwards towards the sea: and it stood there still, as Herodotus says, in his own time.

Otherwise he does not say much about Cyrene itself. It is less than absolutely certain that he ever actually went there, but the balance of the evidence swings over very strongly in favour of the probability that he did. His unambiguous statement that the statue of Aphrodite still stood there in his own time hardly contributes anything to it. He could quite easily have ascertained this by questioning men from Cyrene in the ports and cities of Egypt, and in the length of time he spent in Egypt he could easily have met and talked to enough of them to make him confident that their statements about the statue, since they all agreed, must be true.

Of somewhat greater weight is his description of the place where Battus and his companions first settled on the mainland of Africa before the Libyans persuaded them to move further west. This has an immediacy which is never present in his hearsay descriptions: "a place called Aziris, a charming spot, with a river on one side and lovely valleys on both". Herodotus, the arch-sceptic and non-aesthete, is not in the habit of describing valleys as lovely or spots as charming unless he has actually seen them. Mythical customs he may describe from hearsay, but mythical charm and loveliness he does not.

The most positive evidence, however, is that of his information about the tribes to the south. He divulges also a great deal of information about the tribes further west, but these are obviously hearsay accounts. They are brief, tend to be vague and are mostly composed of strange improbabilities. The tribes south of Cyrene are described in a quite different manner, with a fullness and exactitude that can only have been conferred by his seeing them for himself. The contrast between the hearsay and the eye-witness account is nearly always easy to perceive, and never more so than here, where the two are so closely juxtaposed. In a hearsay account, Herodotus will speak of the cattle of the Lotophagi, who have to walk backwards as they graze, because their horns bend forwards and downwards in such a way that if the cattle moved forwards they would stick in the ground. But he will never speak—as he does—of the Libyan women who are addicted to the practice of wailing at religious ceremonies and, moreover, "do it beautifully", unless he has heard it for himself. Another man may or may not be reliable on matters of fact, but on matters of aesthetic judgment he is inherently and inevitably unreliable, since ultimately the only basis of aesthetic judgment which can be trusted to match with one's own is one's own.

The Greek colonists were settled along the fertile strip of coast that stretched from south of Benghazi in the west to south of Derna in the east. It was a crescent running round that bulge of the coast, an arc perhaps two hundred miles long from one end to the other. Its centre was occupied by a tableland which descended to the sea in a series of steps. The climate of the coastal terraces was agreeable, sheltered as they were by the mountains behind from the hot winds from the Sahara, and open to the cool sea-breezes from the north. The soil was rich and well-watered by streams running down from the mountains to the sea, so that vegetation, including crops and fruit-trees, flourished. The region was as good for the production of cereal crops, Herodotus says, as any land in the world. The soil was black and irrigated by springs; there was no fear of drought, on the one hand, or of damage from excessive rain—though in this part of Libya rain was not unusual—on the other. The yield from harvests equalled that of Babylonia. Above all, the fertile strip had the rare privilege of three harvest seasons. The crops near the coast were the first to ripen. As soon as the harvest was brought in, the crops in the middle region, the first terrace of the hill country, were ready for harvesting, and when these had been harvested those in the highest terrace were ripe. In this way the men of Cyrene enjoyed a harvest season which from beginning to end occupied eight months of the year. The only drawback was the periodical visitations of locusts.

South of the fortunate coastal belt lived the nomad tribes. All these nomads, from the borders of Egypt in the east to the Gulf of Syrtis in the west, followed a similar way of life. The Gulf of Syrtis was the great bay to the west of Cyrenaica, where Tripolitania begins, and where a harsher country reaches right down to the sea. It is called now the Gulf of Sidra; there is a town called Sirte on the coast, between El Agheila and Buerat el Hsun, and the country on its south, the coastal region of Tripolitania, is called Sirtica.

The nomads of Cyrenaica lived on meat and milk. They did not breed pigs, and abstained from eating cows' meat for religious reasons, like the Egyptians. By implication, therefore, the meat they ate was that of sheep and goats. Even the townswomen of Cyrene, Herodotus says, thought it wrong to eat cows' meat, and refrained from doing so out of respect for the Egyptian Isis, whose fasts and festivals they celebrated.

The nomads were the healthiest people in the world, the only people healthier than the Egyptians, as Herodotus says elsewhere. They themselves attributed this excellent health to certain rather bizarre customs observed in the bringing up of their children. For instance, when the children were four years old the parents burned the veins on their heads, and sometimes on their temples, by lighting pieces of greasy wool and applying them to the veins. If this practice happened to bring on convulsions, they sprinkled the child with goats' urine. This, Herodotus says, is what the nomads themselves told him, but whether it was really the reason for their excellent health he was not prepared to say, though of the health itself there was no doubt.

When the nomads sacrificed to their gods, the first step was to cut off the victim's ear and throw it over the house as a preliminary offering, and then to wring the animal's neck. They sacrificed to the sun and the moon, and some of them, those further west, to Athena, Triton and Poseidon. Herodotus was of the opinion that the Greeks had copied the "aegis", the snake-edged goatskin worn by Athena, from the dress of the Libyan women, since there was no difference between them except that the dress of the Libyan women was of leather and had fringes of leather thongs instead of the border of snakes that distinguishes the aegis of Athena. What he says of the dress of Libyan women does not, it seems, altogether correspond to the aegis, except that, as the name implies, the latter was basically goatskin. The goatskins worn by the Libyan women had, unlike the aegis, been stripped of their hair and dyed red, and had those fringed edges that he mentions. He also believed that the wailing of women at Greek festivals was copied from Libyan women, since they do the same, and do it beautifully. Herodotus is exceptionally appealing in his readiness to believe that almost everything the Greeks did they learned from someone else, often the most unlikely people; it is in refreshing contrast to the practice of the present day, when virtually every nation in the world can confidently name the man who invented the flying machine or the telephone and claim him as one of their own.

The nomads buried their dead lying flat, as the Greeks did, except for one tribe who buried them sitting up, and took care when someone was dying to make him sit up to do so. Their houses were made of the dried stems of some plant, bound together with ropes plaited from rushes, and were, of course, portable.

Of these tribes Herodotus speaks with the authority of personal observation; but of those further to the west, as he himself says, "my knowledge fails". He asked many questions in Cyrene concerning the country and the tribes further west, as far as the Pillars of Hercules and beyond, and the information he gathered provides a number of amusing stories, but there is little of real substance in them. It is interesting to try to trace correspondences between these more or less weird fictions and what may have been the truth but, what with imagination on the one hand and speculation on the other, little emerges of any reality that can be relied on. Perhaps the most agreeable story—and one that contains at least a shred of real geography— is that of the country adjoining Mount Atlas, a mountain which is a slender cone in shape and is so high that the top can never be seen, because it is never free from cloud either in summer or winter. The people living around it are called Atlantes, after the mountain, which they call the Pillar of the Sky. They were said never to eat any living creature, and never to dream.

To the south of the coastal belt where the nomads live was a waterless desert, without rain or trees or animal life, or a drop of moisture of any kind, from either wells or dew. Herodotus was eager to confirm, if he could, his persistent theory that the Nile must flow from west to east through the country beyond the desert, before turning north to enter Egypt; since only in this way would it mirror the course of the Danube in Europe. There was a yearning among the ancient geographers to establish this kind of symmetry in their picture of the world, and Herodotus, despite his mocking disbelief in the great, world-circling stream of Ocean, was not immune from it.

There are stories from the west of wild men and women, fabulous animals and some animals less than fabulous, such as lions, elephants, bears, asps and horned asses, but, as he says, in the nomads' country none of these occurred. Instead there were white-rumped antelopes, gazelles, deer, and asses, not the horned kind but a different species which could do without water; another kind of antelope as big as an ox, whose horns were used for making lyres; foxes, hyaenas, hedgehogs, wild rams, jackals, panthers, land-crocodiles like huge lizards four and a half feet long, ostriches, and small snakes with a single horn. There were no stags and no wild boars, but three kinds of mice, also weasels, which were found among the silphium, a plant familiar to Herodotus, since the Greeks imported it from Cyrenaica for both food and medicine; it may have been an umbelliferous plant related to fennel.

Cyrene itself was a delightful place, a bustling, prosperous city with its wonderful climate, its situation of unparalleled beauty, and its luxuriant countryside with its almost year-round harvests. It was delightful, too, for Herodotus to be back in a Greek city, where the temples, the streets, the houses, the way of life were those to which he was accustomed. There is still a great deal left of the physical material of the city. The remains are both Greek and Roman, and include streets, aqueducts, temples, baths, gymnasiums, the acropolis, theatres, tombs, fragments of sculpture and an immense subterranean necropolis burrowed into the face of the terrace on which the city stands. They have been extensively knocked about by the operations of time, weather and, above all, man, and the population of the place at a recent count was five hundred.

It was delightful, but it was not the place where he wanted to be. He had been born and brought up in a Greek colony, and had grown tired of it; and Cyrene had not even the rich intellectual life of Ionia as a compensation for its remoteness from the centre of affairs.

He sailed away, eastwards, along the coast. He was not even going straight home; he had some enquiries to make in Tyre. He may or may not have put in at some Egyptian port on the way. Whether he did so or not, the day came when the ship carrying him stood out to sea, and Africa fell away behind him for the last time.

He had heard that there was a temple in Tyre of great sanctity, dedicated to Heracles, and he wished to find out how much truth there was in what the Egyptians had told him, that they had had a god named Heracles from time immemorial. The god was in fact named Khons, but of his identity as Heracles Herodotus is in no doubt. Seventeen thousand years, the Egyptians said, before the time of Amasis twelve gods were produced from the original eight—different kinds of Egyptians had different views, of course, on who these were, and on how many there were of them—and Heracles was one of the twelve.

Tyre was a city of great antiquity, a Phoenician colony founded by men from Sidon, about twenty miles to the north, probably about 1500 B.C. It stood originally on an island, but Hiram, the king of Tyre who advised Solomon about the building of the temple at Jerusalem, connected it to the mainland by a causeway, which grew as silt was deposited until the island became a peninsula, in the same way as Cyzicus in the Black Sea.

There is little left of it now; since the Crusaders gave it up to the Sultan Qalawun in A.D. 1291, after the fall of Acre, the Moslems fairly thoroughly destroyed it and it has never recovered. All that Herodotus cared about there—at least, all he takes the trouble to speak about—is the temple of Heracles, and he does not say very much about that except that it was as ancient as Tyre itself, that Tyre had stood for two thousand three hundred years, and that the temple was adorned with offerings that were both beautiful and valuable, among the most remarkable being two pillars, one of gold, the other of emerald, which in the darkness gleamed with a strange radiance.

The priests confirmed that Heracles was more ancient than the Greeks believed, so taking the same view as the Egyptians. Herodotus found another temple in Tyre dedicated to the Thasian Heracles; and that is all he says about it, or about Tyre.

He sailed away again, past Cyprus and past Rhodes, and threaded the Dodecanese, to come home to port in Halicarnassus.

ATHENS

VI

It was soon clear to Herodotus—if it had not been clear already—that Halicarnassus was no place for him. He was not yet forty, and he still had a long way to go. We know nothing of his family, except for his relation the poet Panyasis, who may or may not have been his uncle, and who had been executed by the tyrant Lygdamis about ten years before. There must have been other relations, and family ties were strong, but few men have ever been prepared to stay where their families are when the course of their lives and their own inner needs demand that they go and live somewhere else. It may have been sheer political unpopularity that was the final cause of Herodotus's leaving Halicarnassus, but everything suggests that his inclination to leave might have triumphed even without it.

His book shows a constant sympathy with Athens and a tendency to take the Athenian point of view. This was the place to present his work, now taking shape, to the public. Within a year or two, and perhaps within a few months, he had said goodbye to whatever relations of his were still living, and sailed for Athens. It was about the year 447 B.C., and he was about 37.

It was a stirring time to visit that city. Its status had leaped in two or three decades from that of a city-state—a powerful one, but one among many—to something like that of an imperial capital. It was bursting with intellectual life. Aeschylus, the father of tragedy, was dead; his trilogy the *Oresteia* had been presented only eleven years before, though he had since died in Sicily at the age of 68. Sophocles was in his late forties; when he was 27 his first play had taken the prize from Aeschylus. It may have been chagrin at this that led the latter to retire to Sicily, where he met his doom, according to an improbable legend, when an eagle dropped a tortoise on his bald head, mistaking it for a stone. Since then Sophocles had held the stage, though the *Antigone* was still some years ahead. Euripides was in his early thirties, and his first play to be seen in public, the *Peliades*, had appeared seven or eight years before. It would not be until 441 that he took the first prize from Sophocles, who in his good-humoured fashion simply went on writing plays: like Verdi, he matured well, and his last play, *Oedipus in Colonus*, was written in his late eighties.

The Ionian philosopher Anaxagoras had preceded Herodotus to Athens, and taught both Pericles and Euripides, but in 450 B.C., when he was 50—about three years before Herodotus arrived—he was accused of impiety by enemies of Pericles and had to retire to Lampsacus. Protagoras, the philosopher from Abdera in Thrace, was about four years younger than Herodotus, and came to Athens at much the same time. Protagoras was the first man to call himself a sophist; the word had no pejorative connotations till Plato hung them on it, and Plato's views on this matter no longer command the universal respect that they once did. Socrates was in his early twenties, working, as his father did, as a sculptor, and was so far unheard of. In the art of sculpture Phidias, who was about 43, reigned supreme.

Athens had been wrecked and burned by Xerxes in 480, but this was more than thirty years ago. Its population is difficult to estimate, but something of the order of 100,000 may not be too far from the mark. Rebuilding was still taking place; there were already some splendid public buildings, but the major task, that of rebuilding the Acropolis, was still in progress. In the first years after the return of the Athenians to their city in 479 much of the former masonry, including many admirable works of former ages, had been ruthlessly swept away, and in the sixties Cimon had overseen the building of the south wall of the Acropolis and the provision of a large level space on the summit that would serve as the platform on which later the Parthenon would be built. After the Peace of Callias in 449 the decision to build a temple to the goddess Athena was taken, and the building of the Parthenon began in 447, about the time of Herodotus's arrival in the city.

The peace with Persia did not by any means bring a solution to the problems of the Athenian empire, rather the reverse. The allies, no longer feeling the need for Athenian protection, began to resist the increasingly irksome domination of that city. A five years' truce with Sparta had been agreed on in 451, but tension was increased again with a Sacred War, when Sparta assisted in freeing Delphi from Phocian rule and the Athenians assisted the Phocians to regain it. There were revolts against Athenian rule in Boeotia, Euboea and Megara. The democratic and expansionist ideas of Pericles were challenged by the conservative and anti-imperialist aristocrats under the leadership of Thucydides, the future historian of the Peloponnesian War. Pericles was not to secure a free hand until the ostracism of Thucydides four years later, in 443.

Pericles was wholeheartedly devoted to securing and extending the power of Athens, and an essential corollary of this was the glorification of Athens herself. In his aim of creating a city worthy to be the centre of the new empire his principal aides were Hippodamus, the architect, and Phidias. Hippodamus's particular talent was the planning of entire towns, and he had first exercised it, under the patronage of Pericles, on Piraeus. The fury of building in Athens was at its height, above all that of the temple of Athena, the Parthenon, and the monumental gateway, the Propylaea, through which it would be approached. Phidias was at work on his gold and ivory statue of Athena for the temple.

Abroad, the hold of Athens on her empire grew tighter. It would not be long before it was decreed that all the allied cities must use Athenian coinage and Athenian weights and measures. The loss of independence this entailed was widely resented, and one state, Samos, refused to accept it. From the Athenian point of view the measure was necessary not only because it increased the control of Athens over the empire, but also because it made the financial resources of the allied cities more accessible. In any empire, the provinces may prosper, but there is an overall tendency for a proportion of their wealth to drain away from the limbs to the centre. The more Athens deprived the cities of the means to defend themselves or the power to rule themselves, the more she had to spend herself on defending and ruling them, and the more she felt it necessary to spend in creating a city worthy of her imperial greatness. The beauty of Athens was exceedingly expensive.

In 446, when Herodotus was still a new arrival in Athens, a thirty years' peace was agreed with Sparta. The duration envisaged was optimistic; in fact the peace lasted rather less than fifteen. It could be said that the terms on which peace was established made war inevitable. Certain states were recognized by both parties, formally and finally, to be allies of Athens, others to be allies of Sparta. The tempting away of an ally by one side from the ranks of the other was no longer a local nuisance to be counteracted by local means, it was a *casus belli*, a threat to the whole structure. The Greek world was divided into two, the democratic sea-power on the one hand and the aristocratic land-power on the other, each with its allies firmly bound to it. The status of the allies of Athens was changing, and it was not long before those one-time allies began to be formally termed "subjects". Their duty was to pay an enforced tribute so that Athens could carry out policies and measures in which they had no say, and embellish the imperial capital with splendours from which, since they could not see them, they derived no apparent benefit.

What Herodotus thought of these historical developments can only be a matter of speculation. He was not an Athenian citizen, though probably he hoped to become one, and since he could in no way influence the course of events his wisest course was to refrain from expressing any views he may have held. He was no political theorist, and history was for him an account of people's actions and their personal motives for performing them, rather than the invention or examination of a set of theoretical concepts designed to justify or explain them. In any case, a pattern that may clearly be seen thirty years later is more often than not invisible at the time. The Persian war he could see, because it was gone by, but he could not be expected to see, any more than anyone else could, the fundamental forces at work in Periclean Athens, and the future disasters to which they would inevitably lead.

Even his views on Pericles as a man and a statesman can only be a matter of informed guesswork. Speculating on them is a wonderful pastime for historians, and a harmless and healthy one, as good as a game of chess or billiards to those inclined for it, but though the skill of the participants is beyond praise and the exercise nothing but beneficial, all that can be said of the results is that at any time one side seems to be winning and another losing, only for the game to swing the other way as the years go by. Once, as has been said, he spoke of him as a lion, and so said in one word as much as was reasonable, since a lion has many admirable qualities and some dangerous ones.

Periclean Athens was a place where life could be lived, more fully, perhaps, than in most times and places in history, by those fortunate enough to live there and possess the means to enjoy it. Those who did not may have enjoyed it less. Though there is no evidence one way or another, it is pleasanter to assume that Herodotus enjoyed it, since his time there was brief. He had been hard at work, on and off, on his history. It was not finished, and he no doubt went on enlarging, amending, revising and adding to it all his life, into his old age, but a lot of it by now was in existence. As ever, he talked to people, and made friends; and men listened to him, and applauded.

After a time—a year or two, perhaps—he was invited to give a public reading, or a series of public readings, of his work. He did so, and according to Plutarch, or to an Athenian historian quoted by Plutarch, the Athenians voted him sixty thousand drachmas as a reward. It is difficult to say how much this corresponds to in modern terms, since there is hardly any kind of correspondence in terms of money between what was needed for life in Athens and life in, say, Carshalton. It might be said, without too much fear of exaggeration, that it was more money than a labourer would handle in a lifetime, since a drachma was a day-wage for a labourer. It was, at all events, a great deal of money, and it was awarded because Herodotus said a lot of things that redounded in favour of Athens, and the Athenians were highly conscious of the value of statements in their favour that were likely to be widely diffused.

He travelled widely, in his lifetime, in many parts of mainland Greece, in Epirus, Thessaly, Macedonia, the Thracian coast and the islands. It is probable that he did so mostly in these few years of his residence in Athens, heartened by the reception of his work and materially aided by the financial reward it had brought him.

Whether he had heard of the law of 451 when he came to Athens it is impossible to say; probably he had not.

In that year, Pericles had a law passed according to which Athenian citizenship was restricted to those whose parents had both been Athenian citizens. His aim in doing so is not wholly clear. It may have been directed in the first place against Cimon, just returned from his exile. Cimon's mother was not Athenian, and Pericles may have thought it a useful measure to have in hand against him. On a wider scale, it would also be a useful weapon against his opponents the oligarchs, since some of them—Thucydides was one—had married foreign women, and their children at least would be rendered un-qualified for citizenship by the law. It was certainly directed only against the rich, since the poorer citizens had little opportunity to meet foreign women, apart from slaves, and it may have been merely an exercise in securing popular support by a measure that appealed to their chronic xenophobia.

Whatever the motive was, the law was in fact little used, and when it was drawn to Herodotus's attention he probably relied on the comfortable thought that it would not be applied to him. He was, after all, of a respectable Halicarnassian family, a man of increasing repute who had been rewarded by the state for his acceptably pro-Athenian attitudes.

The comfort was illusory. It was gradually borne in on him that he had no hope, owing to the law of 451, of ever becoming an Athenian citizen. If he stayed in Athens it must be as a metic, a resident foreigner. This was to deprive him of much of the intellectual life of an Athenian, since intellectual and political life went together as activities of the citizens; and his residence there would never be secure. There was in the city an ever-increasing number of foreigners, who were well on their way to outnumbering the citizens, and there was no guarantee that the Athenians would not one day reject them as undesirable elements of its population.

It was a misfortune and a disappointment, and Herodotus had to set about considering the alternatives to an uneasy residence in Athens as a metic. To return to Halicarnassus was out of the question. He had left it to start a new life because he had had no place there,

and to go back with his tail between his legs as a rejected would-be
Athenian would be intolerable.

One possibility would be to go abroad as a new colonist. Colonies
were still being founded along the Mediterranean coasts, and if he
was prepared to become a citizen of some new *polis*, hacking out its
living on a foreign shore, he would no doubt be acceptable. But he
had come here to get away from a colony, and this new one would
certainly be, during the remainder of his lifetime, a less cultivated and
civilized place than the Halicarnassus he had left.

Pericles, along with his Athenian imperialism, had certain ideas
aimed at reconciling other Greeks to it, and at the same time, of
course, further enlarging Athenian claims to glory. Some years
earlier, during the truce with Sparta, he had had the notion of holding
a Panhellenic congress in Athens. Its aim would be to restore the
temples destroyed by the Persians, carry out the sacrifices of thanks-
giving promised to the gods at the time of Salamis, and affirm the
freedom of the seas. The proposal came to nothing, since Sparta
opposed it, and it had no particular appeal to anyone else; the allied
city-states saw no point in pledging themselves to rebuild Athens
and pay her dues to the gods for her, though that is what they found
themselves doing in the end.

A substitute for this idea soon suggested itself. The new idea was to
send out a Panhellenic colony to Italy to resettle the people of Sybaris,
a city which the colonists of Croton had destroyed sixty years before.
The expedition would be, naturally, under Athenian leadership, and,
as with the abortive Panhellenic congress, Athenian supremacy would
be demonstrated by making her the head of an all-Greek enterprise.
Citizens of any state would be accepted, but the other city-states were
not officially represented, and their citizens would come as individuals
to a city under the aegis of Athens.

The scheme, once decided upon, was introduced with a flourish of
publicity, in which orators, poets, and soothsayers took part. It
appealed to many, and among them was Herodotus. This was another
colony, true, but it was a colony with a difference. Hippodamus, the
architect, was to plan it; Protagoras was to write its laws. He would
be a citizen of the new colony, but an associate citizen, so to speak, of
Athens, and not a Halicarnassian, since Halicarnassus had no voice
in its affairs.

A first attempt at founding a colony to replace Sybaris had been
made in the form of a small expedition in 446. It had come to nothing,
but lessons had been learned. The plan now was to found a city to be
called Thuria (some call it Thurii, but this is the name of its people)
near the site of the old Sybaris. The new colony was a Periclean

foundation and would reflect Periclean ideas, but the will behind it was not purely that of the partisans of Pericles; it received some support also from oligarchs and conservatives.

The second and larger expedition set out in 444 B.C. It is unlikely that Herodotus went with it. He had been only two or three years in Athens. The life there was much to his taste; he was still enjoying the reputation earned by his readings in 446. There were still a great many places round about that he wanted to visit. An intending colonist of Thuria, he felt no urgent need to go and join it. Hippodamus was there already, and there was something to be said for waiting while the town Hippodamus planned got itself, to some extent, built.

There came a time, however, possibly between 443 and 440, when he could delay his departure no longer. It is not to be supposed that he was unduly cast down at the prospect. He was in his early forties, a man of spirit and unquenchable curiosity about the world and its inhabitants. There was good news yet to hear and fine things to be seen, as Chesterton says in the poem. Moreover, he was a travelling man. He had been to the north, the east and the south, about as far in each direction as a man of his place and time could go. Now the time had come to see another corner of the world. The not-so-reluctant colonist said goodbye to Athens and set off for the west, for Italy.

VII

SYBARIS, ON THE Gulf of Taranto—in the instep of the foot of Italy, but nearer the toe—had been founded by Achaean and Troezenian colonists in 720 B.C. Before long it was extraordinarily wealthy, thriving on its trade with the coastal cities of Europe and Asia Minor. Its inhabitants developed a taste for pleasure and luxury so marked that its name has survived ever since as an adjective for those noted for such tendencies.

There were many Greek colonies hereabouts. By 600 B.C. they had become major centres not only of trade but also of the arts and of culture. They formed together the area known as "Magna Graecia", from the extent of their territories, larger than those of the cities of the homeland. They were not, however, noted for unity in action, and wars between the various cities were frequent.

The city of Croton, situated under what might be described as the ball of Italy's toe, sixty miles from Sybaris, was a particular rival. Croton had been founded by Achaeans, assisted by Spartans, in 710 B.C. It became one of the most powerful and flourishing cities in southern Italy. Pythagoras, a native of Samos, settled there some time between 540 and 510, and gathered his disciples about him. There was a famous medical school. Gymnastics were a particular enthusiasm of the men of Croton, and one of its citizens, Milo, was renowned during that period as the greatest of Greek athletes, winning the wrestling at the Olympic Games six times. Much of the supremacy of Croton's athletes was attributed to the disciplines inculcated by the Pythagoreans.

The rivalry between Croton and Sybaris erupted in a series of wars, and in 510 the Crotoniates decisively defeated the Sybarites in battle, with the aid of a Spartan prince. They not only defeated them; they completely destroyed their city, and completed the destruction by diverting into the city the waters of the river Crathis, which flowed into the sea in the vicinity. The exceptional bitterness between the two cities appears to have been exacerbated by, if it was not due to, the contrast between the austere life of Croton and the dissolute life of Sybaris.

The destruction of Sybaris came as a profound shock to the Greek world; it was regarded as morally indefensible. Miletus went so far as to declare a period of public mourning.

Many of the survivors of Sybaris took refuge in other Greek cities, but some remained in the undistinguished small town that grew up among the ruins under Crotoniate rule.

The feeling of outrage at the destruction of Sybaris, though it had occurred so long ago, was in part responsible for the enthusiasm aroused by the Athenian scheme for its re-foundation. The new city of Thuria grew rapidly, not only in its physical structure but also in prosperity and power, aided as it was by the imperial support of Athens. By the time Herodotus arrived there, evidence of the growing success of the scheme was apparent. The city was not without its troubles. It was a rival to Taras, the Greek city known to the Latins as Tarentum and to modern times as Taranto. There were struggles with the indigenous Lucanians and Bruttii. The mixed character of the population caused internal dissent, and elements from other cities than Athens soon began to assert their ascendancy.

However, life there was by no means uninteresting for an observer of human vagaries like Herodotus. He went on quietly working on his book, a process of rearranging, polishing and the bringing in of new ideas springing from the experiences of his travels. It was not Athens, but it had a flavour of its own. There was a greater emphasis on wealth and luxury, but the arts of literature, and particularly of the theatre, flourished. For a very rough and remote parallel, the life and culture of the western Greeks and those of the Greeks of the homeland bore the same sort of relation as those of America to those of Europe; and no lively man who enjoys one can fail to enjoy the other.

After most of a decade had elapsed, Herodotus decided it was time he refreshed himself with a visit to Athens. He returned there in 431; he was 53. He may still have hoped it might prove possible to settle there for good.

Physically, Athens was at the pinnacle of its perfection. The Parthenon was newly completed; Phidias's gold and ivory statue of Athena had been installed in 438. The great building on its rock, in its present battered state, is still a magical spectacle; when Herodotus saw it on his return from Thuria it was gleaming new. It is a notorious fact that in the whole of the Parthenon, apparently simple in its basic design, there is not a single straight line. The effect of a classical serenity of the spirit is conferred by a subtle use of slight curves and inclines; a skilful application of mathematical and optical principles produced a harmony that neither art nor science could have achieved without the aid of the other.

There was little religious feeling about it. Religion was tucked away in the old temple where the ancient wooden statue of Athena Polias stood, the guardian of city and state. Phidias's Athena was the goddess of her worldly triumph.

Despite all the splendour, Athens when Herodotus came back to it was on the brink of tragedy. Political events had been moving with gradual inevitability towards war with Sparta. A complex series of events led up to it, as is true of most wars, but the underlying causes were simple: the pride and lust for power of Athens and Sparta, with Athens the major offender. The conflict was finally sparked off by an event no more world-shaking than an attack by the Thebans on Plataea, the small ally of Athens in Boeotia. The assassination of an archduke at Sarajevo would have done just as well, if there had been any archdukes, and a place called Sarajevo.

Herodotus had written about his own war, the war that was the background of his childhood and youth. He had no wish to write about this one, the background of his elder years. That task was left to Thucydides, a man of vastly different temperament; it would be difficult to find a greater contrast than this between two men of the same nation, following the same profession, both greatly gifted, not far apart in age—Thucydides was thirteen years younger—and yet utterly unalike.

Herodotus stayed in Athens for the rest of 431—Euripides's *Medea* had been produced in the spring of that year—and on into the following year.

In the summer of 430 the plague broke out in Athens. Thucydides himself fell ill of it, but recovered. His account of his symptoms suggests that the disease was in fact typhoid. Its effect on the crowded city was devastating. Corpses littered the streets; it is said that a third of the robust men of military age died, and fatalities among the poor, the ill-nourished, women, children and the old were innumerable. The ravages of the disease continued for two years, and there was another outbreak a little over a year later, in the winter of 427, that lasted another year. By that time Herodotus was, probably, back in Thuria.

Some have said that he died of the plague in Athens. Others have claimed that he fled from Athens to avoid the plague; another way of saying that he left because there was simply no point in his staying, but there are those to whom no opportunity of throwing a dark light on the character of Herodotus is to be missed.

Others have claimed that he must still have been alive in 408 B.C., since there are references in his book to a rising of the Medes against Darius II, which happened in 409, and to the death of the Egyptian

Amyrtaeus, or at least to the restoration to his son Pausiris of his father's kingdom, which would have happened in 408, when Amyrtaeus died, if it happened at all. By that time Herodotus would have been 76. But then, according to Manetho, Amyrtaeus was indeed the sole king of the Twenty-eighth Dynasty, but his successor was Achoris of Mendes, not his son Pausiris, who is, apart from this reference, unknown to history.

Others maintain that, whenever Herodotus died, he certainly did not die in Athens, since he was buried in Thuria, and no one would have shipped his body home in that troubled time, or any other. A Byzantine historian, Stephanus, says that in the market-place of Thuria there was a tomb with an epitaph to Herodotus inscribed on it, saying that he lay there. No trace of this tomb, however, remains, and no other reference to it exists. Some say the Thurii might have put up the tomb in the market-place after some years, for the greater glory of their city, when they found out that Herodotus was still a famous man after his death. But Thuria was not in a particularly flourishing state in those years, and it would have been a rather expensive way of pronouncing in public a fiction that everybody at the time knew to be untrue. And why should Stephanus be eager to invent a tomb, and compose an imaginary epitaph for it? Some people will do anything for money, but to invent tombs and write epitaphs for nothing seems peculiar. Still, people are sometimes peculiar: the inventor of Piltdown Man went to even greater trouble for a no more discernible motive.

On the whole the balance of probability seems to indicate that Herodotus went back to Thuria, and died there. When he died is more difficult to assess, but again the balance of probability seems to indicate that he lived to a fair old age.

As a historian of the Persian war he is accused of many faults, but it is undeniably true that without his account much of its course, many of its incidents and most of the people who feature in it would be utterly unknown. One obstacle to his reputation as a serious historian which many find it hard to overlook is his light-heartedness, a weakness that they cannot forgive, though others may like him better for it. As an observer he was accused of many faults, from inaccuracy and exaggeration to downright lying; it is pleasant that so likeable a man has in quite recent times been so extensively vindicated. Above all he was, and has always been, good company; and although about 2400 years have elapsed since his death, many still find him so.

INDEX